THE TEN COMMANDMENTS
IN RECENT RESEARCH

J. J. STAMM

with

M. E. ANDREW

ALEC R. ALLENSON, INC.
635 EAST OGDEN AVENUE
NAPERVILLE, ILL.

Translated with Additions by M. E. Andrew from the German
Der Dekalog im Lichte der neueren Forschung
(second edition, revised and enlarged)
Verlag Paul Haupt, Bern and Stuttgart, 1962

FIRST PUBLISHED IN ENGLISH 1967
© SCM PRESS LTD 1967
PRINTED IN GREAT BRITAIN BY
ROBERT CUNNINGHAM AND SONS LTD
ALVA

CONTENTS

TRANSLATOR'S PREFACE

In 1958 J. J. Stamm, Professor of Old Testament at the University of Bern, published a small book entitled *Der Dekalog im Lichte der neueren Forschung* ('The Decalogue in the Light of Recent Research'). This first edition appeared as the first number of the series 'Studientage für die Pfarrer. Eine Sammlung von Vorträgen herausgegeben vom Synodalrat der Evangelisch-reformierten Landeskirche des Kantons Bern' ('Study Courses for Ministers: A Collection of Lectures published by the Synodal Council of the Evangelical-Reformed Church of the Canton of Bern'). (A French translation of this edition by Philippe Reymond was published in 1959 by Delachaux et Niestlé of Neuchâtel under the title *Le Décalogue à la lumière des recherches contemporaines*.)

The second revised and enlarged edition of Professor Stamm's book appeared outside the Study Course series in 1962. It is this edition which has been translated here. The 'Additions' which appear at the end of some sections, the longest of which is at the end of the Introduction, pp. 44–75, supplement Professor Stamm's accounts of work done by other scholars. It should be made clear that these are by me. Professor Stamm has read the whole translation, and also the 'Additions', but the responsibility for both is entirely my own. Nor is it claimed that the material has been brought entirely up to date. Work on the subject is going on all the time, and it becomes necessary to make a stop somewhere. Literature which has appeared, or has come to my notice, since January 1965 is mentioned only in the footnotes, or in the Supplementary Bibliography on p. 12.

Thanks are due to the Rev. Professor Thomas F. Torrance of Edinburgh for generous help in a number of matters, and also to the Rev. David J. Kellas of Edinburgh for help in stylistic matters and for finding a large number of English references not available to me here.

Wuppertal-Barmen
November 1965

M. E. ANDREW

7

PREFACE

In the last thirty years, significant progress has been made in the understanding of the Ten Commandments, first as regards the meaning of the Decalogue as a whole, particularly the place which it occupied in the life of ancient Israel, and secondly as regards the precise meaning of the individual commandments, which is continually being brought out more clearly. To give an account of this to those who, although not specialists, are concerned with the matter, seemed to be both a necessary and a worth-while task.

It is not my intention to give an account of the research as such. This would lead to much detail, and I have produced such an account under the title: 'Thirty Years of Decalogue Research.'[1] The purpose here, on the other hand, is to bring out the main lines of development and the fundamental nature of the problems, without seeking completeness in detail.

With the subject 'The Ten Commandments in the Light of Recent Research', it is my intention to keep myself within the bounds of the Old Testament field, and not to deal with those problems in the field of systematic theology which continue to concern us right up to the present time. The reason for limiting myself in this way is not that I regard the parallel endeavours in systematics as unimportant, or even as less scholarly in comparison with Old Testament study! It is only that an equal consideration of the Old Testament and of present-day problems of systematics and ethics goes beyond the scope of one individual. These latter problems are also so weighty that an Old Testament scholar is not able to deal with them in a cursory way. In any case, confining oneself to the Old Testament does not necessarily involve a complete disregard of all questions of systematic theology; for the recent insights into the Decalogue lead from their basis in linguistics and comparative religion into Old

[1] [A translation of the title: 'Dreissig Jahre Dekalogforschung', *ThR*, NS 27, 1961, pp. 189–239 and 281–305. Tr.]

9

Testament theology, and from that into the sphere of systematic theology.

The book is in two parts. The Introduction deals with general topics, such as the question of the transmission of the Decalogue, the problem of its original form and of its origin. Chapter II contains the exegesis of the prologue and of the individual commandments. The book concludes with a retrospective summary.

J. J. STAMM

ABBREVIATIONS

ANET	*Ancient Near Eastern Texts Relating to the Old Testament*, ed. by J. B. Pritchard, 2nd ed., Princeton, 1955
BJRL	*Bulletin of the John Rylands Library*, Manchester
BZ	*Biblische Zeitschrift*, Paderborn
CBQ	*The Catholic Biblical Quarterly*, Washington
Diss.	Dissertation
EHG	*Eucharisterion. Studien zur Religion und Literatur des Alten und Neuen Testaments. Hermann Gunkel zum 60. Geburtstage, 1. Teil*, ed. Hans Schmidt, Göttingen, 1923
ExpT	*The Expository Times*, Edinburgh
ETr.	English translation
EvTh	*Evangelische Theologie*, Munich
FSAB	*Festschrift Alfred Bertholet zum 80. Geburtstag*, ed. Walter Baumgartner *et al.*, Tübingen, 1950
GAT	*Geschichte und Altes Testament* (Beiträge zur historischen Theologie, ed. Gerhard Ebeling, 16), *Albrecht Alt zum siebzigsten Geburtstag*, Tübingen, 1953
GO	Walther Zimmerli, *Gottes Offenbarung. Gesammelte Aufsätze zum Alten Testament*, Munich, 1963
GSAT	Martin Noth, *Gesammelte Studien zum Alten Testament*, 2nd ed., Munich, 1960
HDB	*Dictionary of the Bible*. 2nd ed. Original ed. by James Hastings. Revised by Frederick C. Grant and H. H. Rowley, Edinburgh, 1963
IDB	*The Interpreter's Dictionary of the Bible*, ed. by George Arthur Buttrick *et al.*, New York, 1962
JBL	*Journal of Biblical Literature*, Philadelphia
KS I	Albrecht Alt, *Kleine Schriften zur Geschichte des Volkes Israel* I, Munich, 1953
NS	New Series
OTL	Old Testament Library, London
ThR	*Theologische Rundschau*, Tübingen
ThT	*Theologisch Tijdschrift*, Leiden

Tr.	Translator's note
VT	*Vetus Testamentum*, Leiden
WuD	*Wort und Dienst. Jahrbuch der Theologischen Schule Bethel*, Bethel
ZAW	*Zeitschrift für die Alttestamentliche Wissenschaft*, Berlin
ZThK	*Zeitschrift für Theologie und Kirche*, Tübingen

The figures in bold type at the top of some pages are the page-numbers of the second German edition of the book. Their absence indicates the 'Additions'.

SUPPLEMENTARY BIBLIOGRAPHY

The following books and articles have come to my notice very recently.

E. Auerbach, 'Das Zehngebot—Allgemeine Gesetzes—Form in der Bibel', *VT* 16, 1966, pp. 255–76.

R. Frankena, 'The Vassal-Treaties of Esarhaddon and the Dating of Deuteronomy', *Oudtestamentische Studiën* 14, 1965, pp. 122–54.

H. B. Huffmon, 'The Exodus, Sinai and the Credo', *CBQ* 27, 1965, pp. 101–13.

J. P. Hyatt, 'Moses and the Ethical Decalogue', *Encounter* 26, 1965, pp. 199–206.

J. Jocz, 'Law and Grace, with Special Reference to the Fourth Commandment', *Judaica* 21, 1965, pp. 166–77.

D. J. McCarthy, 'Covenant in the Old Testament: The Present State of Inquiry', *CBQ* 27, 1965, pp. 217–40.

J. H. Meesters, *Op zoek naar de oorsprong van de Sabbat*, Assen, 1966.

E. Nielsen, *Die zehn Gebote. Eine traditionsgeschichtliche Skizze*, Copenhagen, 1965 (ET in preparation).

J. Schreiner, *Die zehn Gebote im Leben des Gottesvolkes*, 1966.

G. M. Tucker, 'Covenant Forms and Contract Forms', *VT* 15, 1965, pp. 487–503.

M. Weinfeld, 'Traces of Assyrian Treaty Formulae in Deuteronomy', *Biblica* 46, 1965, pp. 417–27.

I

INTRODUCTION

1. *The Transmission of the Decalogue*

As is well known, the Decalogue appears twice in the Old Testament, in Exodus 20 and in Deuteronomy 5, and in both cases as a document which is directly connected with and central to the revelation at Sinai. In addition to these two versions, there is a third, the so-called Nash papyrus, which was acquired in Egypt in 1902 and published in England in 1903.[1] This is a sheet of papyrus dating from about 100 BC, which gives the Decalogue and the passage Deut. 6.4 f in Hebrew square characters without vowels. The wording of the Decalogue sometimes corresponds to the version of Ex. 20 and sometimes to that of Deut. 5. It thus represents a late combination of no value as an independent tradition of the text, and I shall therefore give no further consideration to it in what follows.

The question of the Qumran texts also arises in this connection. Here it can be said that they have hardly produced anything of value for the text of the Decalogue as yet. Among the fragments found in 1949, there are some of Exodus and Deuteronomy, but those of Deuteronomy give nothing from the Decalogue, and those of Exodus nothing more than the beginning (Ex. 20.1): 'And God spoke all these words, saying.'[2] It is certain that the picture will be changed once the numerous tiny fragments of biblical texts which were discovered in 1952 in another cave near Qumran are published.

In the meantime, it is still necessary to keep to the Old Testament versions of the Decalogue in Ex. 20 and Deut. 5. These

[1] The text is reproduced in Ernst Würthwein, *The Text of the Old Testament*, ETr., Oxford, 1957, p. 92.
[2] See D. Barthélemy and J. T. Milik, *Qumran Cave I*, Oxford, 1955, p. 51.

differ in over twenty points. Thirteen of them are additions which Deuteronomy has over and beyond Ex. 20. Seven of these are, however, merely the connecting particle w^e 'and', and it is not necessary to give the references where this occurs in Deut. 5 and not in Ex. 20. The remaining, more important additions may, however, be mentioned. Both the sanctification of the sabbath and the honouring of parents are strengthened in Deuteronomy by the sentence: 'as Yahweh your God commanded you.' In the list of those who are to benefit by the sabbath rest, the Deuteronomist inserts 'your ox and your ass' before 'your cattle', and, he also writes not simply 'your cattle' but 'all your cattle'. In addition, he concludes the list of those favoured by the sabbath rest with the sentence: 'that your manservant and your maidservant may rest as well as you.' Finally, in the commandment concerning parents, he has enriched the pledge of long life in the promised land with the words: 'and that it may go well with you.'

Apart from three minor differences in the wording of the second commandment,[3] those still remaining are as follows. In the fourth commandment, Exodus reads 'Remember the sabbath day', while Deuteronomy has 'Observe the sabbath day'; the reason given for the same commandment in Exodus is that God rested on the seventh day, while in Deuteronomy the people are reminded of their slavery in Egypt and of their deliverance. In Exodus, the ninth commandment reads: 'You shall not appear as a lying (*šeqer*) witness against your neighbour', and, in Deuteronomy: 'You shall not appear as a false (*šāw'*) witness against your neighbour.' In the tenth commandment, the word order of Exodus ('your neighbour's house—your neighbour's wife') is reversed in Deuteronomy, and the second *lō'-taḥmōd* ('you shall not covet') of Exodus is replaced in Deuteronomy by the form *w^elō' tit'awwe* (from the verb *hit'awwā*, 'desire', 'lust after').

As far as I can see, the only one of these differences on which no certain judgement can be given is that at the beginning of the sabbath commandment, i.e.: 'Remember the sabbath day' or 'Observe the sabbath day'. For is 'observe' really the appropriate

---

[3] For 'You shall not make yourself a graven image, or any likeness' in Ex. 20.4, Deut. 5.8 has 'You shall not make yourself a graven image of any likeness.' To the words 'to the third and fourth generation' in Ex. 20.5 correspond '*and* to the third and fourth generation' in Deut. 5.9. Ex. 20.6 has 'my commandments', whereas the *k^etīb* of Deut. 5.10 offers 'his commandments'.

term, as Koehler thinks,[4] while 'remember' presupposes a longer existence of the institution and is therefore secondary? Or is it, as Eduard König thought,[5] just the opposite, that 'remember' is the older term which, since it easily admitted of excuse, was then replaced by the stricter 'observe'?

Of the reasons given for the sabbath rest, that of Deut. 5 is the older since it is stamped by the spirit of Deuteronomy, while that of Ex. 20, with its probable connection with the Priestly account of creation, will be the younger.[6] As far as the other differences are concerned, the opposite can be said. The text of Deuteronomy represents a somewhat later version; its deviations from Exodus reveal modernizing tendencies. This is particularly true of the additions in Deut. 5, since they betray a desire for more precision in content and greater rhetorical fulness. This striving for more precision is probably the reason why the 'lying witness' of Exodus has been replaced in Deut. 5 by 'false witness', since one who was called a 'false witness' could not claim, as one who was called a 'lying witness' perhaps could, that he had not actually told a lie. It is certainly also a modernizing intention, giving more consideration to the position of the individual, which has led to Deuteronomy mentioning the wife before the house, so that she is distinguished from the property of her husband which is listed in what follows. Since Hebrew favours a slight variation of expression in repetitions, the choice of *lō' tit'awwe* in Deuteronomy in the same commandment, instead of *lō'-taḥmōd* as in Exodus, must be understood as a stylistic improvement. When we come to the exegesis of the tenth commandment, we shall then see that the change in the choice of words probably also indicates a somewhat different understanding of the conception of coveting.

As has been indicated already, the facts just mentioned lead to the conclusion that a somewhat more ancient version of the Decalogue is preserved in Ex. 20 than in Deut. 5. However this

[4] L. Koehler, 'Der Dekalog', *ThR*, NS 1, 1929, p. 180.

[5] E. König, *Das Deuteronomium*, Leipzig, 1917, p. 92.

[6] It is striking that the last words of Ex. 20.11 do not correspond exactly with Gen. 2.3. Karl Budde, *Die biblische Urgeschichte*, Giessen, 1883, pp. 492 ff, has concluded from this that the Priestly document was not the first to have known the resting of God after creation as the reason for the sabbath rest. Gottlob Schrenk in his article 'Sabbat oder Sonntag?', *Judaica* 2, 1946, pp. 169 ff, refers to Budde and agrees with him (p. 176). Others, however, take a different view, e.g. E. Jenni, *Die theologische Begründung des Sabbatgebotes im Alten Testament*, Zollikon, 1956, p. 20.

judgement is valid only for their respective traditions and not for their final written form. For, as far as the latter is concerned, the connection which seems to exist between the Sabbath commandment of Ex. 20 and the Priestly document makes it possible that the Exodus text in its written form is later than that of Deuteronomy. The assumption that the later text preserves an older form of tradition than the earlier one is by no means impossible; the Priestly document, for example, in its elaborate cultic character shows more archaic features than the Yahwist, who is much freer as regards the cult.

With its more ancient form, the version of Ex. 20 is closer to the original than that of Deut. 5. Despite this, however, just how far even Ex. 20 is removed from the actual original is shown by the fact that it, as well as Deut. 5, is preserved in deuteronomistic language. This can be seen both in the introduction, with its designation of Egypt as 'house of bondage', and also in individual expressions in the explanatory clauses in the second, fourth and fifth commandments.[7] They make the linguistic connection with the deuteronomistic circle certain.[8] Deuteronomy as a whole can be dated as a work of the seventh and sixth centuries BC, and this means that it is to this rather late time that the form of the Decalogue which has come down to us probably belongs. This fact alone would settle every question concerning the age and origin of the Decalogue if it contained deuteronomistic language only. But this is not the case.

As we have seen, the reason given for the Sabbath commandment in Ex. 20, with its echoes of the Priestly account of creation, is an element which is later than Deuteronomy. The predominant elements, however, are those which show no sign at all of deuteronomistic style and which have no connection with the Priestly document; they are thus evidently older than either of these. They consist mainly of those clauses which, in contrast to the explanatory clauses, form the nucleus of the commandments; but we should also notice one passage from the explanatory

[7] These are brought together by Hans Schmidt in 'Mose und der Dekalog', *EHG*, p. 85.

[8] Henning Graf Reventlow in *Gebot und Predigt im Dekalog*, Gütersloh, 1962, pp. 14 ff, thinks that the correspondences mentioned are due not to the linguistic dependence of the Decalogue additions on the deuteronomistic circle, but to the Decalogue being in the course of time absorbed into the stream of Deuteronomy's expository preaching of the earlier law.

clauses to the second commandment: 'for I Yahweh your God am a jealous God, visiting the iniquity of the fathers upon the children to the third and fourth generation (of those who hate me), but showing steadfast love to those who love me (and keep my commandments).' These clauses on the jealousy of Yahweh and on his retributive action take up two old confessional formulae,[9] the second of which, indeed, contradicts the spirit of Deuteronomy in its inclusion of the sons and grandsons of the guilty person. For Deuteronomy (24.16) restricts punishment, as far as human justice is concerned, to the guilty person himself without bringing it to bear on his sons, and sees divine retribution as effective directly in the life of every individual (7.10).

ADDITIONS

A consideration of the meaning of Deut. 5.20 in comparison with Ex. 20.16 ('false [*šāw'*] witness' and 'lying [*šeqer*] witness') is left over until we come to the discussion of the ninth commandment in detail.[10]

Some further remarks of Reventlow's may be added. He says[11] that both versions, although handed down in two different literary complexes, show agreement in those clauses which form the nucleus of the Decalogue, and that this is an eloquent sign of the reliability of a tradition which goes back to very old foundations. As already mentioned, Reventlow[12] does not think that the additions to the Decalogue come from the deuteronomistic circle, at least not as the product of a literary process. Form-critically, the Decalogue stands in the closest proximity to Deuteronomy since both are 'preached law', but this does not mean that both are to be traced back to the same authorship, but that both share a common place of origin. Later,[13] he states his case even more strongly: the different layers which can be distinguished in the Decalogue are not the result of particular sources or of literary circles, but they are stamped by their place of origin, the Festival of the Covenant, in which various interests were represented. Referring to the promise of long life which, in the

---

[9] On this, see W. Zimmerli, 'Das zweite Gebot', *FSAB*, p. 555 = *GO*, p. 239.

[10] See below, pp. 110 f.   [11] *Gebot und Predigt*, pp. 9 f.

[12] *Ibid.*, pp. 13 ff.   [13] *Ibid.*, p. 40.

fifth commandment, is related to the giving of the land by Yahweh,[14] Reventlow affirms that, apart from its use in the fifth commandment, it occurs word for word only in Deuteronomy, and appears there frequently. This cannot, however, be used to support the thesis of the deuteronomic origin of the Decalogue, for, in reality, the concern of preaching itself leads in this direction, a preaching which later came to perfect expression in Deuteronomy. Reventlow still thinks, however, that the Decalogue in Deuteronomy is the later version,[15] since the process of homiletic amplification has gone a step further there, and since the understanding of the content of some commandments has moved away from their original meaning.

The difficulty with this thesis is whether preaching on the clauses of the Decalogue actually did take place within the Festival of the Covenant. Some are even going as far as to raise questions about the Festival of the Covenant itself![16]

2. *The Problem of the Original Form*

The distinction which has been drawn between a deuteronomistic framework and a pre-deuteronomistic nucleus raises the question of the original Decalogue. The answer has not been sought merely in the elimination of the deuteronomistic elements, but the short form of the sixth, seventh and eighth commandments has at the same time been taken as a model, and attempts have been made to fit the remaining commandments to this model. This principle forms the basis of the reconstruction which, for example, Rudolf Kittel[17] has made; it reads as follows:

I.   I Yahweh am your God: you shall have no other gods beside me.

II.   Do not make yourself a divine image.

[14] *Gebot und Predigt*, pp. 67 f.   [15] *Ibid.*, p. 95.

[16] These questions and the question of the connection between the commandments themselves and the Festival of the Covenant are discussed in detail below, pp. 46 ff and 66 f.

On the additions to the Decalogue, see also J. Weingreen, 'Exposition in the Old Testament and in Rabbinical Literature', *Promise and Fulfilment. Essays Presented to Professor S. H. Hooke*, ed. by F. F. Bruce, Edinburgh, 1963, pp. 190 ff; also, on the subject of both this and the following section, see the recent article by N. Lohfink, 'Zur Dekalogfassung von Dt 5', *BZ*, NS 9, 1965, pp. 17–32.

[17] R. Kittel, *Geschichte des Volkes Israel* I, 6th ed., Gotha, 1932, pp. 383 f.

III. Do not utter the name of your God Yahweh for empty purposes.[18]

IV. Remember the sabbath day, to keep it holy.

V. Honour father and mother.

VI. Do not murder.

VII. Do not commit adultery.

VIII. Do not steal.

IX. Do not speak lying witness against your neighbour.

X. Do not covet the house of your neighbour.

In this series where prohibitions predominate, the commandments on the sabbath and on reverence towards parents stand out because of their positive form. It seems likely that they too could once have had a prohibitive form, and scholars like Sellin[19] and Alt[20] have allowed for this possibility. The resulting version of the fourth commandment reads: 'You shall not do any work on the sabbath.' The step taken in the case of the fifth commandment is a little more far-reaching, since the insertion of another verb is necessary to make a prohibition. Corresponding to the old clause: 'Whoever curses his father or his mother shall be put to death' (Ex. 21.17), this will probably have been 'curse', *qillēl*. Following this, the fifth commandment will probably have once run: 'You shall not curse your father or your mother.' Since the positive wording was more suited to the subject matter, it is easy to understand that it replaced the negative in both the fourth and the fifth commandments. In the case of the fifth, Reventlow[21] also reckons with such a re-wording, but since he sees the fourth coming from priestly and not from legal (apodictic) tradition like the others, he considers it possible that this was always positively formulated.

The attempts mentioned completely exhaust the possibilities provided by the text of the Decalogue and, in the case of the fifth commandment, by a related ancient statute. It is therefore doubtful whether there is justification for going further, since one then necessarily departs from what is given by the text, and enters the sphere of pure hypothesis. However, Karlheinz Rabast,

---

[18] *Führe den Namen deines Gottes Jahwe nicht für Nichtiges im Munde.*

[19] E. Sellin, *Geschichte des israelitisch-jüdischen Volkes* I, Leipzig, 1924, p. 84.

[20] A. Alt, 'Die Ursprünge des israelitischen Rechts' (hereafter cited as 'Ursprünge'), *KS* I, pp. 317 f.

[21] *Gebot und Predigt*, pp. 54 ff and 63.

a pupil of Albrecht Alt, has made such an attempt[22] in which he makes use of his teacher's form-critical insights. (I refer to these shortly.) Like Alt, Rabast assumes that the oldest Hebrew statutes were worded metrically, and, as a basis for the Decalogue, clauses which each have four stressed syllables can be recognized from the second, third, ninth and tenth commandments. It is finally postulated that a first table also containing six clauses corresponded to the second table of the Decalogue with its six clauses beginning with the commandment concerning parents. The Decalogue (= ten words) would thus have been originally a dodecalogue (= twelve words). The reconstruction composed by Rabast with these presuppositions has the following form:

I.   I, Yahweh, am your God.
II.   You shall have no other god beside me.
III.   You shall not make yourself an image.
IV.   You shall not worship them (god and image).
V.   You shall not misuse my name.
VI.   You shall not do any work on the sabbath.
VII.   You shall not curse your father and your mother.
VIII.   You shall not kill a man in his person.[23]
IX.   You shall not commit adultery with the wife of your neighbour.
X.   You shall not steal a man or a woman.
XI.   You shall not be a false witness against your neighbour.
XII.   You shall not covet the property of your neighbour.

It is not my intention to go into a detailed critical discussion of this attempt at reconstruction now. It serves merely as an example of how much the question concerning the original Decalogue is still in a state of flux, and to what novel solutions it can lead. The fact that there are several of them shows too that the form of the original Decalogue will never be recovered decisively down to the last word. That does not hinder us, however, from concluding that there was a Decalogue in Israel which must have been older than Deuteronomy, and which contained ten statutes which were recognized as basic.

[22] K. Rabast, *Das apodiktische Recht im Deuteronomium und im Heiligkeitsgesetz*, Berlin, 1949, pp. 35 ff.

[23] *Du sollst nicht einen Menschen an seiner Seele töten*. Rabast has here inserted the Hebrew word *nepeš*, 'person', 'self' into the text of the commandment: *lō' tirṣaḥ 'iš nepeš*.

ADDITIONS

In connection with the taking of the short form of the sixth, seventh and eighth commandments as a model for reconstructing the original Decalogue, Erhard Gerstenberger[24] says that verbs used absolutely in the negative in the shortest form are not very numerous. Only the Decalogue has really valid examples of this kind (Ex. 20.13,14,15 = Deut. 5.17,18,19), and he thinks that the Masoretic verse division has mistakenly made too much of the separation between them. When Deuteronomy joins the second and third prohibition of this series with w^e, 'and', it is possibly preserving an older feature, and this allows the conclusion that the short prohibitions once belonged together more closely (cf. also Deut. 5.20,21). All other examples of the short form (except perhaps for Lev. 19.26b) are doubtful, as a supplementary object always occurs in connection with them (see Lev. 19.11,13a,18a; Deut. 14.1; even Lev. 19.11a). Thus, if in these examples a closer defining of the prohibitions by all kinds of grammatical additions seems to be necessary, even this formal matter supports the view that the 'absolute' prohibitions did not always have a universal meaning, but rather a concrete one within known social structures. The verbs in the absolute prohibitions of the Decalogue are all more closely defined by some addition when they come to be more precisely used, and it is only their emotional content and assumed context which make the absolute use possible at all. It will thus be necessary, as a rule, to supplement the verb, and this necessity could be avoided only in particular cases where the prohibitions were especially transparent. The shortest form cannot be seen as the classical one; Ex. 20.13 ff represents rather a whittling away of forms which were once more precise.

Pierre Buis and Jacques Leclercq[25] maintain that neither of the two versions of the Decalogue can be the source for the other, but that they both derive from the same original which must have been confined to short formulae. By comparing the two texts and comparable lists, they too think that they can give an idea of this original, which they write in italics in their translation. It is as follows: '*I, Yahweh, am your God who led you out of the land of*

---

[24] E. Gerstenberger, *Wesen und Herkunft des 'apodiktischen Rechts'*, Neukirchen, 1965, pp. 73 f (cited hereafter as *Apodiktisches Recht*).
[25] P. Buis and J. Leclercq, *Le Deutéronome*, Paris, 1963, pp. 63 ff.

Egypt; you shall have no other gods before me; you shall not make yourself any image; you shall not utter the name of Yahweh lightly; observe the sabbath day to keep it holy; honour your father and your mother; you shall not kill; and you shall not commit adultery; and you shall not steal; and you shall not make a false testimony against your neighbour; and you shall not covet the wife of your neighbour, the house of your neighbour, or anything that is your neighbour's.'

However, in the light of Gerstenberger's remarks above, the reconstruction of the absolutely original form on the basis of short clauses becomes problematic, though their retention of 'and' from the seventh commandment onwards is interesting. In the case of the tenth commandment, however, this particular lengthy form is difficult in the light of Stamm's remarks below.[26]

F. H. Woods and B. J. Roberts[27] point out that the Hebrew texts of Ex. 20 and Deut. 5 agree in the order 'murder, adultery, theft' in the sixth, seventh and eighth commandments, but that the best manuscripts of the Septuagint have the order 'adultery, theft, murder' for Exodus, and 'adultery, murder, theft' for Deuteronomy. They think that the last may possibly have been original since it is borne out by Luke 18.20; Rom. 13.9, and by the Nash papyrus and Philo.

3. *Age and Origin of the Decalogue*

How old are the statutes which existed before Deuteronomy, and, to put the question more specifically, is it possible that they go back to the time of Moses, or even perhaps that they come from his own hand? This question leads us to give some consideration to the history of the Decalogue problem in Old Testament studies.

In the period from about 1880 until 1910, the leading critical scholars were convinced that Mosaic authorship was impossible and that the Decalogue was late, that is, that it was at the very least dependent on the ethical demands of the great prophets. Julius Wellhausen set the tone; according to him, Moses had given no law which was valid once and for all, although he had for forty

---

[26] P. 101 and n. 76.
[27] Article 'Ten Commandments', *HDB*, p. 970a.

years proclaimed law at the sanctuary.[28] Wellhausen was followed
by his friends and pupils, men like Bernhard Stade, Karl Budde,
Rudolf Smend and Karl Marti.[29] The last-mentioned scholar also
denied that Moses had legislated; he did not give his people a fixed
law, but rather something greater, namely religion with an ethical
tendency. With few exceptions,[30] it was only decidedly conservative scholars like August Dillmann, Eduard König and Rudolf
Kittel[31] who still believed at that time that they were able to claim
that the Decalogue was very old, or even that Moses was its
author.

The critical voices already mentioned continue to make themselves heard in the period from 1910 to 1930. The majority of
critical scholars like Carl Steuernagel, Carl Heinrich Cornill,
Johannes Meinhold, Wilhelm Nowack and Gustav Hölscher[32]
continue to hold the view that the Decalogue must be late, that is,
post-prophetic if not even exilic or post-exilic. But now there is no
longer any unanimity among the critically inclined as there was
formerly. A breach into their front was made by Hugo Gressmann

[28] J. Wellhausen, *Prolegomena to the History of Israel*, ETr., Edinburgh, 1885,
p. 369. Here Wellhausen stresses that this is the conception of the narrative
of Ex. 18, and remarks that the Torah belongs in the story as Moses' pro-
fessional activity, and not as a codex. See also his *Sketch of the History of Israel
and Judah*, 3rd ed., London, 1891, pp. 18 ff; Bruno Baentsch, *Exodus-Leviticus-
Numeri*, Göttingen, 1903, pp. 178 f, and Heinr. Holzinger, *Exodus*, Freiburg,
1900, pp. 77 f.

[29] Stade, *Biblische Theologie des Alten Testaments* I, Tübingen, 1905, pp. 248 f;
Budde, *Geschichte der althebräischen Literatur*, Leipzig, 1906; also his
Religion of Israel to the Exile, ETr., New York, 1899, pp. 31 f; Smend,
Lehrbuch der alttestamentlichen Religionsgeschichte, 2nd ed., Freiburg, 1899,
pp. 17 ff, and especially p. 40; Marti, *The Religion of the Old Testament*, ETr.,
London, 1907, pp. 63 ff.

[30] So B. D. Eerdmans, 'Ursprung und Bedeutung der zehn Worte', *ThT* 37,
1903, pp. 19–35; Gerrit Wildeboer in *Theologische Studien*, 1903, pp. 109–118;
also his *Die Literatur des Alten Testaments*, Göttingen, 1905, pp. 16–22.

[31] Dillmann, *Exodus und Leviticus*, 3rd ed., Leipzig, 1897, pp. 219 f; König,
'Neueste Verhandlungen über den Dekalog', *Neue Kirchliche Zeitschrift* 17,
1906, pp. 565–584; Kittel, *History of the Hebrews* I, ETr., London, 1895,
pp. 244 f.

[32] Steuernagel, *Lehrbuch der Einleitung in das Alte Testament*, Tübingen, 1912,
pp. 259–261; Cornill, *Introduction to the Canonical Books of the Old Testament*,
ETr., London, 1907, pp. 80 ff; see also his *Zur Einleitung in das Alte Testament*,
Tübingen, 1912, pp. 24 ff; Meinhold, *Der Dekalog*, Giessen, 1927, pp. 7, 106
and 196; Nowack, 'Der erste Dekalog', *Abhandlungen zur semitischen Religions-
kunde und Sprachwissenschaft. Wolf Wilhelm von Baudissin zum 26. Sept. 1917
überreicht*, ed. by W. Frankenberg and F. Küchler, Giessen, 1918, pp. 381–397;
Hölscher, *Geschichte der israelitischen und jüdischen Religion*, Giessen, 1922, p. 129.

who, in his book on Moses,[33] deviated boldly from the opinions
widely held at that time. He doubted, for instance, whether the
lack of cultic elements in the so-called 'ethical Decalogue' of
Ex. 20 is really sufficient reason for considering it to be later than
the so-called 'cultic Decalogue' of Ex. 34, since, in the history of
religion, ethics is not later than the cult. It is not probable that
the 'ethical Decalogue' is dependent on the prophets, since the
concern with social questions which is characteristic of the prophetic ethic is lacking in the original form of the Decalogue. In the
light of Israel's sojourn at Kadesh, no objections can be raised
to the 'houses' of the tenth commandment, and the sabbath is an
ancient institution borrowed from the Midianites. Finally, the
prohibition of images, despite all the later transgressions, fits into
Mosaic religion which was imageless, having as its symbol the ark
representing an empty divine throne. Gressmann does not hesitate, therefore, to define the Decalogue of Ex. 20 as the 'catechism
of the Hebrews in Mosaic times'. He adds, however, that scholarship has made probable (not proved) only that the document
originated in the time of Moses, and we are not able to judge
whether Moses was personally involved in it or not. In a work
which appeared later,[34] Gressmann gives up the early dating
mentioned, and maintains that the basic material of the Decalogue
goes back to the tenth or the ninth century. This means that it
would still be pre-prophetic or early prophetic, but it would have
originated only in Palestinian times, and not in Israel's early
nomadic period.

In spite of this, Gressmann's earlier view has had a strong
influence. This can be seen in the case of Hans Schmidt, who
expressed himself very confidently on this matter in his contribution to the Gunkel *Festschrift* in 1923.[35] According to him,
Moses is really the author of the Decalogue. He gave it to the
Israelites on Sinai, and its text, inscribed on two tablets of stone,
was kept in the ark for centuries.

Like Gressmann in 1913, Ludwig Koehler also makes a
cautious judgement in his account of research on the Decalogue
published in 1929.[36] He maintains that by critical work a much

[33] *Mose und seine Zeit*, Göttingen, 1913, pp. 473 ff.
[34] *Die älteste Geschichtsschreibung und Prophetie Israels*, 2nd ed., Göttingen,
1921, p. 237.
[35] 'Mose und der Dekalog', *EHG*, pp. 78–119.
[36] 'Der Dekalog', *ThR*, NS 1, 1929, pp. 161–184.

older Decalogue can be won from Ex. 20 and Deut. 5 which contains nothing 'that makes its composition in the time of Moses impossible'. But to attribute it to Moses himself is not possible 'since each Decalogue is impersonal in its literary composition'.

With these quotations from Gressmann, Schmidt and Koehler, we have presented the judgement of three prominent critical scholars for the period from 1910 to about 1930. But they stand alongside other critical scholars of that time who, now as before, were of the opinion that the Decalogue had a late origin. The opinions in favour of Mosaic authorship have obviously grown more numerous in comparison to earlier times, even if, at least in the critical camp, they still do not form a majority.

The situation is different in the period after 1930. There are certainly still some scholars who attribute the Decalogue to a later time, and who see in it a prophetic-priestly compromise,[37] but those who advocate such views are in a minority. They have against them a strong majority who reckon with the extreme antiquity of the Decalogue at all events, if not indeed with its Mosaic origin. Anyone who examines the question more carefully has to make a distinction here, since the antiquity of the Decalogue is advocated much more generally and more decidedly than its Mosaic authorship. The latter view is naturally taken by those who reject modern biblical criticism and who believe that they are able to attribute the Pentateuch in the main to Moses. This is the case with the Dutchman G. C. Aalders, a strict Calvinist, who published a short introduction to the Pentateuch in 1949,[38] and also with the profound Jewish thinker André Neher.[39] Mosaic authorship of the Decalogue is also accepted unreservedly by those who do not completely reject biblical and particularly pentateuchal criticism but whose view of it lies between the reserved and the critical. This is the case with Martin Buber who, in his book on Moses,[40] makes full use of the Decalogue as a genuine Mosaic

---

[37] So Adolphe Lods, *Histoire de la littérature hébraique et juive*, Paris, 1950, pp. 335 ff, 357 ff, and especially 365 f; Robert H. Pfeiffer, *Introduction to the Old Testament*, London, 1952, pp. 228 ff; Georg Beer, *Exodus*, Tübingen, 1939, pp. 103 f.

[38] G. C. Aalders, *A Short Introduction to the Pentateuch*, London, 1949; similarly in Wilhelm Möller, *Grundriss für Alttestamentliche Einleitung*, Berlin, 1958, pp. 52–54 and 107 ff.

[39] A. Neher, *Moses and the Vocation of the Jewish People*, ETr., London, 1959.

[40] M. Buber, *Moses*, London, 1946.

document. It is also true of Roman Catholic scholars, some of whom have gone into the subject very thoroughly.[41]

But even among Protestant scholars who assent to the critical results of Old Testament studies, there are those who confidently attribute the Decalogue to Moses, e.g. Paul Volz, Harold H. Rowley and Walther Eichrodt. Volz's book on Moses appeared in a first edition in 1907. At that time, he sought to find a picture of Moses and his work chiefly by drawing conclusions from the post-Mosaic and pre-prophetic epoch. The Decalogue played no great part in this; it was even maintained that whether Moses promulgated it or not was unimportant compared with the fact that he was the creator of an ethical religion.[42] But the second edition of the book, in 1932, takes a completely different line. Now, the Decalogue is seen as the 'programme of the Mosaic legacy', not only as *a* word of Moses, but as *the* word which we have from him.

In an article which appeared in 1951,[43] Rowley has gone into a thorough discussion of the objections which had been brought against the Mosaic origin of the Decalogue. He cannot see that any of these holds good, and he is of the opinion that the so-called 'cultic Decalogue' of Ex. 34 comes from the time before Moses. It is probable that this is the old Decalogue of the Kenites which the southern tribes of the later Israel had then handed on. Moses gave the later middle Palestinian groups which were led by him the 'ethical Decalogue', taking over some clauses from the older Kenite document.

In 1953, Eichrodt joined in the discussion of our problem.[44] He sees in Moses the leading figure of the early period during which rational, political as well as formal, cultic action is not yet separated from direct inspiration and from action stemming from enthusiasm and momentary possession. It was Moses' task to give precise regulations and basic principles to the people whom he led. These are found in the Decalogue and in the Book of the Covenant, though certainly in a form which has been distorted considerably by tradition.

[41] So Andreas Eberharter, *Der Dekalog*, Münster, 1930.
[42] Volz, *Mose*, 1st ed., Tübingen, 1907, p. 84.
[43] H. H. Rowley, 'Moses and the Decalogue', *BJRL* 34, 1951–52, pp. 81–118 = *Men of God*, London, 1963, pp. 1–36.
[44] See his article on the religion of Israel in *Historia Mundi*, vol. II, Bern, 1953, pp. 377–448.

In Volz, Rowley and Eichrodt we have scholars who are confident in their judgement concerning the origin of the Decalogue. Very many of their colleagues, however, do not go so far as that, for, while they may think that they can allow for the antiquity of the Decalogue, and from there, for the possibility of Mosaic authorship, they do not go so far as to regard it as certain. Indeed, no less persons than Albrecht Alt and Martin Noth tend to be critically inclined here, since, while they consider the Decalogue to be old, they do not think it is the oldest deposit of Israelite law.[45]

After what has just been said, it is clear that the growing agreement among scholars which, in comparison with earlier times, is astonishing, applies more to the age of the Decalogue in general than to its origin in particular. This doubtless represents a change over to a more conservative point of view which is no longer very far from biblical tradition. This could be a reason for breaking out into Werner Keller's well-known cry of triumph.[46] Whoever is so inclined may do so. I must say I am not; for in this question, it is not a matter of apologetics or of the defence of a particular point of view, but rather one of insight into the Bible through scholarship, which demands of us all continual progress in the subject.

It is therefore our task, with an unbiased attention to the matter concerned, to inquire into the reasons which made possible the change of direction which has been gradually appearing since 1910. Some of these are general, and some particular. The general reasons include a change in the understanding of the beginnings of Israel. It has been recognized that these are not to be seen as completely primitive, as though they were simply analogous to ancient north Arabian polydaemonism, and that the further development of Israel and its resistance to Canaanite nature religion after the Conquest remain incomprehensible if there was not at the beginning a spiritual impulse of considerable proportions. When the beginnings of Israel are understood as less primitive and thus more spiritual, it is seen that observance of the sabbath as well as imageless worship of God were possible. This

---

[45] Alt, 'Ursprünge', *KS* I, pp. 321 f; Noth, *The History of Israel*, ETr., 2nd ed., London, 1960, pp. 103 f; also his *Exodus* (OTL), ETr., London, 1962, pp. 167 f.

[46] W. Keller, *The Bible as History*, ETr., London, 1956. See my critical review in *Kirchenblatt für die reformierte Schweiz* 112, 1956, Nos. 23 and 24.

removes two fundamental arguments which have so often been brought forward against Moses as the author of the Decalogue. In addition to this, the old assertion that the prophetic spirit influenced the Decalogue has lost its force since Gressmann's book on Moses of 1913. For, as we have seen, Gressmann had observed that no trace of the social ethic which is integral to the message of the prophets is to be found in the original Decalogue.

These are the general reasons, to which those of a special nature can be added. They are connected with a great scholarly movement, the beginnings of which, as far as the Decalogue is concerned, fall in the year 1927. At that time, the well-known Norwegian scholar, Sigmund Mowinckel, published his book *Le Décalogue*. This has 162 pages of which more than half contains nothing which could have caused any particular sensation, since the usual questions concerning sources[47] and the age of the Decalogue are dealt with. Further, the question of age finds an answer which for that time was by no means sensational, since Mowinckel places the document in late pre-exilic times, and sees it as a product of prophetic influence, to be more exact of the activity of the disciples of Isaiah. It is not until the second half—from p. 114 on —that we come to those sections which have given the book its fundamental and lasting value.

As has already been stated, Mowinckel thinks that the Decalogue as it has come down to us is late, but this does not apply to the literary type to which it belongs. It can be older, and this insight makes it possible to inquire about the 'origin of the Decalogue'. This is found in the cult, to be more exact in the New Year and Enthronement Festival, the existence of which Mowinckel believed he had demonstrated in the second volume of his famous studies on the Psalms.[48] In order to demonstrate the cultic origin of the Decalogue, he advanced the following theses:

[47] Mowinckel (*Le décalogue*, Paris, 1927, pp. 19 ff) is of the opinion that Ex. 34.14–26 is not the work of the Yahwist, but that he inserted it into his narrative. The statutes of the covenant as given by the Elohist are to be found not in the Decalogue but in the religious, cultic regulations of Ex. 20.23–26; 22.28–29(30); 23.10–19. The Decalogue of Ex. 20 is a later interpolation into the work of the Elohist. In an article 'Zur Geschichte der Dekaloge', *ZAW* 55, 1937, p. 227, Mowinckel gives the following list of Horeb laws in the Elohist's work: Ex. 20.23–26; 22.(17–27),28–29; 23.1–3,6–8(9); 23.10–12,13b–15a,16,18–19.

[48] *Das Thronbesteigungsfest Jahwäs und der Ursprung der Eschatologie*, Oslo, 1922; reprint, Amsterdam, 1961.

1. The Sinai pericope (Ex. 19–24), transmitted by the Yahwist and the Elohist, has its place in the cult; that is, it is nothing other than the description of a religious festival. The idea of a theophany probably also has its origin in the cult, and the reading of the commandments, which were thought of as the expression of the divine will, probably belonged to the festival as well.[49]

2. The New Year and Enthronement Festival had at the same time the function of a Feast of the Covenant, to be more exact of a Feast of the Renewal of the Covenant.[50]

3. The nature and content of the festival can be inferred from other Old Testament passages besides the Sinai pericope. Such are Pss. 81 and 50 with their reference to the situation of the festival together with theophany and proclamation of law. Another passage which is drawn into the argument is Deut. 31.10–13, with its prescription that the deuteronomic law be read before men, women and children every seven years at the Feast of Tabernacles at the beginning of the Year of Release. Mowinckel stresses that this passage is late, but that it preserves the memory of a much earlier usage, in which, at one time, other and much shorter collections of law had been recited at the Feast of Harvest and of the Covenant. Such a reading took place originally every year and not every seven years.[51]

4. It is a cultic prophet who is seen as the one who proclaimed the law at the festival, which reminds us that the third volume of Mowinckel's studies on the Psalms was entitled: 'Cult Prophecy and Prophetic Psalms.'[52]

5. The Israelite festival began with the interrogation of those attending concerning the conditions of participation. This is a situation from which the Pss. 15 and 24, known as Entry Liturgies, have grown. The decalogues, at least in their main features, are connected with these. Here, as a prescription for entry into temple and cult, they have their *Sitz im Leben*. Originally their content

---

[49] *Le décalogue*, pp. 120 f.   [50] *Ibid.*, p. 123.   [51] *Ibid.*, pp. 124 ff.
[52] [My translation of the title: *Kultprophetie und prophetische Psalmen*, Oslo, 1923; reprint, Amsterdam, 1961. Tr.] See *Le décalogue*, p. 129.

would have been only cultic and ritual, but it came to be extended when later examples of the type no longer contained prescriptions for entry to a single location of the cult, but gave rules concerning the presuppositions of belonging to the covenant people in general. In this extension, the genre finally came under prophetic influence, and it is this which forms the spiritual background of the Decalogue which has come down to us.[53]

By these arguments Mowinckel has probably proved decisively the connection between Decalogue and cult, and with this he has lifted the research into the Decalogue on to a new level. For, over and beyond all considerations of literary criticism, he has opened up the possibility of seeking the function of the Decalogue in the life of ancient Israel. Mowinckel has provided a fruitful impulse even if he has raised more questions than he has answered. Of all these, we mention only two. Firstly: does the recognition of the cultic structure of the Sinai pericope justify the assumption that its whole content has come out of the cult? Is it not more likely that an extremely ancient, pre-cultic and historical element was preserved in the cult, and that it was then transmitted and probably also formed by it?[54] And secondly: can such a close connection as Mowinckel wishes really be seen between the Decalogue and the Entry Liturgies like Pss. 15 and 24? If this is done, it leads to the conclusion that the proclamation of the will of God stood at the beginning, and therefore on the edge of the Israelite festival, and not at its central point. But enough of questions.

Instead of more questions, it is our task to trace the activity which the impetus of Mowinckel has brought about in later scholarship. Here one soon comes upon the famous essay of Albrecht Alt which has already become classical. It is on the origins of Israelite law, appeared first in 1934, and is reprinted in the collection of Alt's most important shorter writings on the history of the people of Israel.[55] Here, Alt transfers to Old Testament legal literature the form-critical method which Gunkel had tested on the Genesis sagas, prophetic sayings and the psalms,

[53] *Le décalogue*, pp. 141 ff.
[54] So G. von Rad, *Das formgeschichtliche Problem des Hexateuch*, Stuttgart, 1938, pp. 19 f; ETr. in *The Problem of the Hexateuch and Other Essays*, Edinburgh and London, 1966, pp. 21 f.
[55] *Die Ursprünge des israelitischen Rechts*, Leipzig, 1934 = *KS* I, pp. 278-332.

and finds in it two forms: the pronouncement formed conditionally with a main and a dependent clause, and the short imperative or prohibitive clause. He calls the first kind casuistic law, and the second apodictic law. Casuistic law is to be found particularly in the many 'if-clauses' of the Book of the Covenant (Ex. 20.22–23.19), and besides this in Deuteronomy and also in the Holiness Code (Lev. 17–26). Agreements in style can be found in the ancient oriental legal documents which are known from Sumerian times on,[56] and its content also shows many contacts with them. It is therefore not to be doubted that Israel took over this so-called casuistic law from her Canaanite neighbours after the Conquest. Its place in the life of the people was in the local jurisdiction formed by the men of the villages and the towns.[57] To the Israelites coming from the desert this law was new at first, and, for this reason, it needed to be cultivated with particular care. This was a responsibility which was handed over to the bearers of an office which pertained to all Israel. Alt thinks that these officials were the so-called 'minor judges', of whom the Book of Judges (10.1–5; 12.7–15) only tells us, along with information about their place of residence and burial, and occasionally about their family, that they judged the people for so many years. As distinct from the 'major judges', who were war heroes inspired by the spirit, these were legal functionaries, a kind of spokesman to speak the law like those in ancient Iceland, whose function was the transmission, preservation and exposition of the law taken over in Canaan.

Apodictic law has come down to us in several series which combine the single short commands or prohibitions. The best

[56] The following documents exist: the codex of Urnammu of Ur (c. 2050 BC), the law book of Lipit-Ishtar of Isin (perhaps the first half of the nineteenth century BC), the laws of Eshnunna (probably about 200 years older than the laws of Hammurabi), the codex of Hammurabi (usually dated c. 1730–1688, but probably to be placed earlier in the time about 1900), the Middle Assyrian laws (from the twelfth century BC), the Hittite laws (the copy preserved comes from the last years of the Hittite Empire, about 1200 BC, but the original was considerably older), the New Babylonian laws (from the time of the New Babylonian Empire, 626–539). With the exception of the first, these texts are brought together and translated in *ANET*, pp. 159b ff; see also W. F. Albright, *Recent Discoveries in Bible Lands*, New York, 1955, pp. 35 f, and Hartmut Schmökel, *Kulturgeschichte des alten Orient*, Stuttgart, 1961, pp. 154 ff.

[57] On this, see L. Koehler, 'Justice in the Gate' (first published in German in 1931, and now reprinted as an appendix to the book *Hebrew Man*, ETr., London, 1956).

known among these is the Decalogue of Ex. 20 and Deut. 5. A second series, likewise readily recognizable, is the collection of twelve crimes to be cursed which is preserved in Deut. 27. This latter has an importance going beyond its form and content in that it preserves a situation to which apodictic law belonged. This was the assembly of the people, that is, assembly of the people in the ancient sense, involving the men who accepted legal, military and cultic obligations. The assembly was 'in the large amphitheatre between Ebal and Gerizim in the pass of Shechem'.[58] Here the Levitical priests recited the clauses, and the congregation of the people had to take each curse upon itself with a loud Amen.

Three further series of apodictic laws are less easily and less certainly recognized, since they come to us in a form which is no longer always connected, and they are also mixed with other legal material. The first of these, a series of crimes punishable by death, is found by Alt[59] in Ex. 21.12,15–17; 22.18 and 19; 31.14 f. In it are to be found clauses like: 'Whoever strikes a man so that he dies shall be put to death', 'Whoever curses his father or his mother shall be put to death'; 'Whoever sacrifices to other gods shall be utterly destroyed'; 'Whoever does any work on the sabbath day shall be put to death'—this latter according to the reconstructed text of Ex. 31.14 f.[60] Probably clauses from Lev. 20.2,9–13,15–16, 27; 24.16; 27.29 also belong in this series; they are concerned with sacrifice to Moloch, cursing of parents, lying with animals, illicit kinds of sexual intercourse, necromancy, and with the misuse of the name of Yahweh.

A second series of apodictic laws which cannot be recognized immediately is to be found in Lev. 18.7–18 in the form of a twelve-member list of the degrees of relationship in which sexual intercourse is not permissible.[61] Finally, a series which can be gathered from Ex. 22.17,20,21,27; 23.1–3,6–9 (Lev. 19.15 f) is to be placed alongside the one just mentioned. It has to do with certain 'taboo' figures—divinity, stranger, widow, orphan, ruler—in relation to whom certain actions are to be performed, or to be omitted.[62] The first series mentioned is formulated in the third person, but the last two series by contrast come close to the Decalogue with their use of the direct address 'you': 'You shall not revile God, nor curse a ruler of your people.'

[58] Alt, 'Ursprünge', p. 324.   [59] *Ibid.*, pp. 310 ff.   [60] *Ibid.*, p. 311, n. 3.
[61] *Ibid.*, p. 315.   [62] *Ibid.*, pp. 315 f.

It may be thought surprising that the so-called 'cultic Decalogue' of Ex. 34.14–26 does not figure among the collections of apodictic law. Alt left it out purposely since he did not consider it to be an ancient and original legal corpus, but only a 'secondary mixed formulation'.[63] Several scholars have followed him in this opinion, while others still believe that they are able to sift out an ancient decalogue from this context.[64] A decision for one or the other is difficult. We may leave the matter where it stands.

In its form, apodictic law is without parallel in ancient oriental law, and its content is permeated with the spirit of the religion of Yahweh. The exclusive claim of the divine Lord of the covenant is essential to it—the Lord who has singled out for himself a people who are not to be touched by the immoral customs of their environment. From the point of view of this characteristic, Alt's assumption that apodictic law is a genuine expression of the Israelite people is attractive, and what can be learnt about the 'setting in life' of the people in which this law was proclaimed fits in with it. This situation was not, as in the case of casuistic law, the 'secular' life of the village, but rather the festival. To prove this, Alt[65] quotes the apodictically formulated table of curses in Deut. 27 which gives information about a situation presupposing a solemn ceremony near Shechem. Like Mowinckel, he also considers Deut. 31.10–13, though he evaluates the passage more accurately and does not immediately look for a connection with the hypothetical Enthronement Festival. After the Decalogue has found its home among related documents of apodictic law, it is no longer possible, as Mowinckel wished, to place it alongside the Entry Liturgies known from the Psalter. Alt keeps exactly to the information given by Deut. 31.10–13, seeing it as preserving the memory that a legal text much shorter than Deuteronomy was read out at the central point of the Feast of Tabernacles every seventh year at the beginning of the Year of Release. Pieces of that circumstantial and detailed law, which were secular and

[63] *Ibid.*, p. 317, n. 1.

[64] Representatives of both points of view are noted in Rowley, 'Moses and the Decalogue', *BJRL* 34, 1951–52, p. 90, n. 1 = *Men of God*, p. 9, n. 1, and in W. Beyerlin, *Origins and History of the Earliest Sinaitic Traditions*, ETr., Oxford, 1965, p. 81, n. 282. In contrast to Alt, M. Noth, *Überlieferungsgeschichte des Pentateuch*, Stuttgart, 1948 (reprint, Darmstadt, 1960), p. 33, seems to reckon with the possibility that an ancient decalogue can be reconstructed from Ex. 34; see also his *Exodus*, pp. 262 f.

[65] 'Ursprünge', p. 325.

casuistic, do not come under consideration as the legal texts which were used for such a purpose in ancient times, though apodictic ones certainly do. And that, from among these, the Decalogue itself was actually used, is shown by Psalm 81 'which according to its hymnic introduction is evidently meant for the Feast of Tabernacles, and which then soon changes to speech put into the mouth of Yahweh and proceeds to the recitation of the first clauses of the Decalogue'.[66]

The Feast of Tabernacles in ancient Israel was at the same time the New Year Festival, and was thus bound up with thoughts both of beginning anew and of remembrance. This was even more true of every seventh year, when the Feast of Tabernacles coincided with the beginning of a Year of Release, to which belonged the land's sacral time of lying fallow and the suspension of special legal procedures. These measures were evidently intended to bring the Israelite people back to the normal state of their life in the seventh year after all the failures of the preceding six. If texts of apodictic law were read out on this occasion, this means, as Alt states,[67] 'a leading back of the community to the ideal foundation of its life, a new engagement of all members to the will of Yahweh. . . . Though it may not be usual to express the matter thus [in the Old Testament], this recitation of apodictic law at the Feast of Tabernacles every seventh year which bound the whole congregation of the people, is simply a regularly repeated renewal of the covenant between Yahweh and Israel which, according to their own conviction, had called them into existence'. Alt adds[68] that, under these circumstances, it cannot be a matter for surprise that the writers of the Hexateuch preferred to insert the series of apodictic laws into the complex of the narratives concerning the first covenant at Sinai. For, since these series 'were regularly used in the acts of the renewal of the covenant and in this situation could only be understood, and were only meant to be understood, as the fixed expression of that divine will which was always the same and which had always applied in the covenant of Yahweh with Israel, it was thus an almost self-evident conclusion that they would have been expressed in the same wording at the making of that first covenant'.

It follows from this sentence that Alt sees the connection of apodictic law with Moses and with Sinai grounded in the cultic

[66] 'Ursprünge', p. 330.   [67] *Ibid.*, p. 328.   [68] *Ibid.*, p. 329.

practices of Israel, to be exact, in the recitation of law in the Feast of Tabernacles. The question whether a historical fact lies at the basis of this, in other words, the question whether Moses himself may be claimed as the creator of particular maxims of apodictic law, is not directly answered. However, an indirect answer is given when he maintains[69] that the foundations of the form of apodictic law were laid in the desert even if the formulations of the type which are preserved for us did not originate there, but in Canaan. It was here, in the pre-monarchic period of Israel, in the time of the judges, that the genre had its creative period. These general considerations show that, for Alt, it is impossible to believe in a Mosaic origin of the Decalogue. To these can be added special reasons which follow from a comparison of the Decalogue with other documents of apodictic law. Among them, series predominate in which particular transgressions limited to single spheres of life are brought together—the so-called special series. Only the table of curses in Deut. 27 and the Decalogue are of a comprehensive nature. The Decalogue is distinguished from the former, as well as from other series, by its categorical clauses containing no definitions of punishment. It also lacks any reference to particular cases. With the help of these observations, Alt forms the opinion that the Decalogue is more likely to be a late example of this type.[70] In this he is in agreement with Martin Noth, who states[71] that the religious and moral prohibitions of Ex. 22.17 ff have most right to be considered elements of the original Israelite divine law.

4. *Prospect*

Alt's essay on the origins of Israelite law is without doubt the most important contribution to the understanding of the Decalogue since Mowinckel. He has shown the place which it occupied in ancient Israelite life, setting it in its literary context by classifying it as apodictic law, and in its cultic context by connecting it with the Feast of Tabernacles. Insights have thus been won which are fundamental, though they are, of course, certainly not definitive. Questions still remain, and answers are being given which do not always correspond to what Alt believed he had been able to establish. As a conclusion to the first part of this survey,

---

[69] *Ibid.*, p. 330.   [70] *Ibid.*, pp. 321 f.   [71] *History of Israel*, p. 104.

attention is drawn to such questions and problems. As far as I can see, the following can be specified:

1. The first question is the one posed by Alt himself[72] concerning the law which the ancestors of Israel had in the time before they became members of the amphictyony of twelve tribes. Perhaps it will never be possible to give a certain answer to this, and yet there does exist a collection of texts from which an answer ought to be sought. They are the cuneiform tablets from Mari on the middle Euphrates which come from the time of Hammurabi.[73] They are written in Babylonian, but in this Babylonian there are some early Hebrew words,[74] as well as names which are conformable to names in later Israel. Evidently we meet here the earliest ancestors of such groups which, along with others, were later to become the Israelite people. But it is not only in the sphere of language that there are clear kinship relations between these ancestors and later Israel, for the fact that an early form of prophecy existed here shows that there were also relations of a religious nature.[75] If there are connections in this sphere, is it not also possible that there were some in law? That the specifically Hebrew, non-Babylonian word for 'judge' [šōpēṭ] also occurs in Mari texts may be an indication of this. The question, therefore, is one of defining more closely, if possible, the function of these judges in Mari.

2. Who recited the apodictic laws at the Feast of Tabernacles? Alt did not pay any particular attention to this question. In any case, he did not think of the 'minor judges', whose importance as legal personages he had recognized, since he saw in them the transmitters and expositors of casuistic law. Noth[76] has put forward the opposite view to this: the 'minor judges' had nothing to do with casuistic law; rather, they were the bearers of apodictic law and those who proclaimed its clauses at the festival. The expression

[72] 'Ursprünge', *KS* I, p. 330.
[73] On the dating of this king, see above, p. 31, n. 56.
[74] These are brought together in M. Noth, *Die Ursprünge des alten Israel im Lichte neuer Quellen*, Cologne, 1961, pp. 34 ff.
[75] On this, see M. Noth, *Geschichte und Gottes Wort im Alten Testament*, Krefeld, 1949 = *GSAT*, pp. 230–247 = 'History and the Word of God in the Old Testament' (slightly shortened), *BJRL* 32, 1949–50, pp. 194–206.
[76] 'Das Amt des "Richters Israels"', *FSAB*, pp. 404–417.

'judge of Israel' which occurs only once in the Old Testament (Micah 4.14), is the ancient designation of their office. This conception has been extended, and even possibly carried too far, by Hans-Joachim Kraus.[77] He thinks that there was the special office of a 'mediator of the covenant' (*Bundesmittler*) in Israel for the reading out of the apodictic legal clauses, and that the 'judge of Israel' was the bearer of this office. (In the revised edition of his book,[78] Kraus expresses himself more cautiously on the matter.) That the 'minor judges' had to do with law may be regarded as settled, but it is difficult to make out whether their business was either casuistic or apodictic law, especially as the 'either . . . or' could also be replaced by a 'both . . . and'. The reason why it is not certain that the 'minor judges' recited the apodictic law is because the priests can also be considered for this function. It is of them that Zimmerli thinks, on the grounds that the first words of the Decalogue are rooted in priestly tradition.[79]

3. What was the construction of the ancient Tabernacles–Covenant Festival which, according to Deut. 27 and Josh. 24, was celebrated in Shechem? Alt, whose chief point was that the recitation of law stood at the central position of the sacral celebration,[80] only made suggestions on this second question, but von Rad has gone further in a work of fundamental importance.[81] Stimulated by Mowinckel, he recognizes in the basically similar construction of the Sinai pericope and of Deuteronomy the structure of an ancient liturgical formula. Basing himself on Josh. 24, he outlines its elements and goes on to reconstruct the ancient festival as follows:[82]

(i) Exhortation or parenesis (according to Josh. 24.14 f a call to the undivided worship of Yahweh).

---

[77] *Gottesdienst in Israel*, Munich, 1954, pp. 59 ff.

[78] 2nd ed., Munich, 1962, pp. 128 ff; ETr., *Worship in Israel*, Oxford, 1966, pp. 108 f.

[79] 'Ich bin Jahwe', *GAT*, pp. 179–209 = *GO*, pp. 11–40; see also Zimmerli's commentary *Ezechiel*, Neukirchen (still appearing in fascicles), pp. 397 ff. Rabast in *Das apodiktische Recht im Deuteronomium und im Heiligkeitsgesetz*, Berlin, 1949, pp. 38 f, also thinks of the priests as the spokesmen of apodictic law. On the other hand, H. Reventlow in *Wächter über Israel*, Berlin, 1962, pp. 116 and 124 f, considers a prophet as the spokesman.

[80] 'Ursprünge', *KS* I, p. 326.

[81] *Das formgeschichtliche Problem des Hexateuch*, Stuttgart, 1938, pp. 23 ff = *The Problem of the Hexateuch*, pp. 26 ff.

[82] See also von Rad, *Old Testament Theology* I, ETr., Edinburgh, 1962, pp. 192 f, and H.-J. Kraus, *Worship in Israel*, pp. 13 f.

(ii) Consent of the people (Josh. 24.16 f, 24: 'Yahweh our God we will serve, and his voice we will obey').

(iii) Proclamation of the law (Josh. 24.25: 'So Joshua made a covenant with the people that day, and made statutes and ordinances for them at Shechem').

(iv) Making of the covenant, or renewal of the covenant (Josh. 24.27: setting up of a stone of witness).

(v) Promise of blessing if the statutes are kept, and announcement of curse if they are transgressed (Deut. 27.12; Josh. 8.34).

We may therefore believe that we have found some traces not only of the festival to which the Decalogue and related texts belonged, but also of the position which the reading out of the law occupied within it. It may be noted in addition that the Sinai pericope, Deuteronomy and also Josh. 24 all show us that the paranesis which stands at the beginning followed a review of the history of salvation, just as when the Sinai events as a whole were related at the Feast of Tabernacles, the proclamation of law had as its background the recapitulation of the history of salvation.

4. Alt contrasted the Decalogue, with its comprehensive content and its generalized clauses which mention no punishment, with series of apodictic law which mostly have particular spheres of life as their subject matter, and which also mention punishment of one kind or another. He considered these so-called special series to be the earlier phenomenon, and the Decalogue to be an early, but in comparison with these, a later fruit on the tree of apodictic law. The possibility of attributing the Decalogue to Moses thus seems to be out of the question. But another opinion is possible concerning the relation of the comprehensive, so-called collective series like the Decalogue and the table of curses in Deut. 27 to the special series mentioned. For is it necessary that the special series stood at the beginning of the development, and that the collective series came only afterwards as it were as a synopsis? Is not the opposite development also conceivable, that the collective series formed the beginning and that the special series broke away from them? Karlheinz Rabast, in his book already mentioned, thinks that the process took place in this way.[83] This must certainly be considered seriously, and from that

[83] *Das apodiktische Recht im Deuteronomium und im Heiligkeitsgesetz*, pp. 39 f.

standpoint, the consideration that Moses was the author of the Decalogue would no longer be excluded as a matter of course. Is it not preferable and better to ascribe the Decalogue, which is a collective series extracting the essential from many subordinate series, to that pre-eminent personality Moses, rather than to a later unknown author? Personally, I do not hesitate to do the first; and whoever is not prepared to do this must at least acknowledge, as von Rad does,[84] that the Mosaic authorship of that original Decalogue which has been freed from secondary additions can neither be proved nor disproved by scholarship. Whatever one thinks about the authorship, the fact that the Decalogue, together with other documents of apodictic law, early held a central position in Israelite life remains as the most important result of recent research. These documents had their place in the festival, and stood in association with the review of the Sinai events as the binding charter expressing the will of the divine Lord of the covenant.

5. For Albrecht Alt it was essential to contrast casuistic law, which was common to the Orient and taken over by Israel, with apodictic law as a genuinely Israelite creation.[85] He did not think of seeking extra-Israelite parallels to apodictic law and to the form of the festival at which it was recited. This question waited a long time until the American scholar G. E. Mendenhall took it up in two articles which appeared in 1954, and which were published together as a pamphlet in the following year.[86] Here Mendenhall drew attention to treaties which kings of the Hittite Empire in Asia Minor had made in the fourteenth and thirteenth centuries BC with regents who were not their equals in rank (as well as with others). These have been called 'vassal treaties', and in some of them it is actually princes of Syrian peoples who are the partners.[87]

[84] *Old Testament Theology*, I, p. 18, n. 9.   [85] See above, p. 33.
[86] *The Biblical Archaeologist* 17, 1954, pp. 26–46 and 49–76; *Law and Covenant in Israel and the Ancient Near East*, Pittsburgh, 1955.
[87] They have been published in the original with a (German) translation by Joh. Friedrich, *Staatsverträge des Chatti-Reiches in hethitischer Sprache, 1. Teil*, Leipzig, 1926, *2. Teil*, Leipzig, 1930, and by Ernst F. Weidner, *Politische Dokumente aus Kleinasien. Die Staatsverträge in akkadischer Sprache aus dem Archiv von Boghazköi*, Leipzig, 1923. As a sample of such a treaty, that of the Hittite Mursilis II (1334–1306) with a king of the Syrian state Amurru is printed in Klaus Baltzer, *Das Bundesformular*, 2nd ed., Neukirchen, 1964, pp. 186 ff. [There are English translations of some of them in *ANET*, pp. 199a ff, and in D. J. McCarthy, *Treaty and Covenant*, Rome, 1963, pp. 181 ff. Tr.]

In general the treaties have the following construction:[88]

(i) Preamble and historical review, i.e. statement of the relations as they existed earlier between the Hittite Empire and the ancestors of the treaty partner.

(ii) Conditions: prohibition of foreign relations outside the Hittite Empire; prohibition of hostile relations with anyone who stands under the sovereignty of the Hittite suzerain; any call to arms by him is to be followed; the vassal must put his whole trust in the Hittite king continually and without reserve; he may not give refuge to any fugitive, and once a year he must appear before the Hittite king (probably for the purpose of paying tribute); disputes between vassals are to be laid before the suzerain for decision.

(iii) Conclusion: a provision that the treaty be deposited in the temple and regularly read out in public; a list of the gods as witnesses; an oath by which the vassal binds himself to obedience, and a list of symbolical, accompanying ceremonies; a symbolical performance of the measures taken against rebellious vassals.

When the three parts of the treaties are compared with the construction of the Israelite festival, to which texts of apodictic law belonged, then the way in which they agree is clear: they both have the historical review, the proclamation of law or of treaty, and the making of the covenant or oath ceremony. There are also correspondences in the content: the condition of the treaties which prohibits foreign relations outside the Hittite Empire reminds us of the first commandment of the Decalogue; other prescriptions from the second part of the treaties, and ceremonies as they are provided for in the third part, correspond more to the account of the making of the covenant in Ex. 24; besides this, the prescription that the vassal must appear once a year before the Hittite suzerain reminds us of the Old Testament cultic regulation in Ex. 23.17 = Ex. 34.23 which stipulates that Israelite men are to appear three times a year before Yahweh, i.e. in the sanctuary of the place concerned, or in the central sanctuary. Mendenhall has drawn attention to these and other similarities,[89] and he thinks

---

[88] See Mendenhall, *Law and Covenant*, pp. 31 ff [and also now the same writer's article 'Covenant', *IDB* I, pp. 714b f. Tr.].

[89] See *Law and Covenant*, pp. 35 ff [and also *IDB* I, pp. 719a ff. Tr.].

that the way in which Old Testament covenants are contracted (besides Ex. 24, see also Josh. 24 and II Kings 23.1–3) stems from the formula of the Hittite treaties. This survived the Hittite Empire (which perished about 1200 BC) among the peoples on the eastern Mediterranean, so that it could have become known in Israel as well. As far as the style of the treaties is concerned, Mendenhall thinks that the same mixture of apodictic and casuistic law is characteristic of them as of the Old Testament Book of the Covenant (Ex. 20.22–23.19). This means too that, contrary to Alt's opinion, apodictic law is not genuinely and exclusively Israelite.[90]

This comes out even more sharply in a Hamburg dissertation by Günter Heinemann.[91] The author says directly that the stipulations of the Hittite vassal treaties show apodictic style, and that an extra-Israelite origin must therefore be accepted. The treaties do indeed contain numerous commands and prohibitions so that it seems likely that they are to be classed as apodictic in form. Like Mendenhall, Heinemann also pays attention to the agreement between the formula of the Hittite treaties and the Old Testament covenant conception. But he does not wish to explain this from a direct Israelite dependence on the Hittite model either. He thinks rather of an indirect connection whereby Shechem, the cultic sanctuary of Baal of the Covenant (Judg. 8.33; 9.4), could be regarded as the connecting link. Besides this, Heinemann also draws attention to the similarity which exists between the construction of the Hittite treaties and that of the ancient Feast of Tabernacles and Renewal of the Covenant in Israel. The form of this festival has its model in the Hittite treaty formula. To quote Heinemann's own words: 'Israel evidently found in this treaty form, which preserves the historical meeting between the treaty partners, the apposite form of expression for her relation with God.'

If Shechem is to be seen as the place at which Israel took over the (originally) Hittite treaty form and the apodictic style belonging to it, then historical consequences follow. It means that the Decalogue cannot be derived from any time earlier than Israel's Canaanite period, neither from the previous nomadic time nor from Moses himself. Walter Beyerlin attempts to avoid this

[90] See *Law and Covenant*, pp. 6 ff [and also *IDB* I, p. 720a. Tr.].
[91] *Untersuchungen zum apodiktischen Recht*, 1958 (typewritten).

conclusion. In doing this he acknowledges the connections which have just been set forth; he even thinks that the Decalogue has been fashioned according to the treaty form known from the vassal treaties of the Hittites, which had become known to the Israelites before they ever came to Canaan.[92] According to him, nothing stands in the way of accepting 'that a primordial form of the Decalogue, as the tradition asserts (Ex. 34.27 f; 24.4,7,12; 20.1), had in fact arisen in the Mosaic period through the use of the treaty form'.[93] Kadesh can be assumed as the place of origin, the place to which, according to Judg. 11.16 f and Ex. 15–18, the groups of the future people of Israel which had fled from Egypt had gone. On a pilgrimage from there, some of them had come to Sinai. It was probably during the stay in Kadesh, which lasted a considerable time, that the juridical and social structure of the Yahweh congregation was organized (according to Ex. 18.13–27). The Decalogue too, as a basic element of the covenant with Yahweh, could already have undergone the first stages of formation here. 'The community of those who had experienced Yahweh's saving activity in the deliverance from Egypt and had encountered his sovereign will at Sinai and had pledged themselves to obey him understood their tie with Yahweh on the analogy of a vassal-covenant. The same treaty form which the Hittite kings had used to make their covenant-will law now became the vehicle for expressing something quite new and unique—the majestic revelation of the nature and will of the God of Sinai. The historical prologue of the Decalogue reminded the Yahwistic community of Yahweh's saving act in delivering them from Egypt and their corresponding obligation of gratitude and obedience; the Ten Commandments themselves contained the demands of the covenant God.'[94]

Though this sounds convincing, it must be stated that it is uncertain whether that type of Hittite treaty could really have already been known to the Israelites at Kadesh. It might well have been more of a possibility for Canaan and especially for Shechem, since the Hittite Empire extended its influence as far as Syria in the fourteenth and thirteenth centuries BC. In this way, cultural elements and legal forms of this empire could have come as far as Canaan, and survived even after the fall of the empire. However,

[92] *Origins and History of the Earliest Sinaitic Traditions*, pp. 54 f.
[93] *Ibid.*, p. 145.   [94] *Ibid.*, p. 146.

it is possible that they may have come as far as Kadesh, since this oasis, according to archaeological finds which have been made there, was not so isolated from the rest of Palestine as could appear from its geographical position. The finds belong to the beginning of the Middle Bronze Age (twenty-first to nineteenth centuries BC), to the time of the Kingdom of Judah, and to the Nabataean–Roman–Byzantine period.[95]

That the nature of the Israelite covenant festival is connected in some way with the Hittite treaty formula can scarcely be contested. As a reminder, we append once again the following four parts of the Israelite festival: 1. Paranetic prologue; 2. Proclamation of the commandments; 3. Making of the covenant; 4. Blessing and curse. The elements from the Hittite treaties which correspond to these are: 1. Preamble and historical prologue; 2. Conditions of the treaty; 3. Conclusion with blessing and curse.

Since the Hittite treaties also contain numerous commands and prohibitions, it is a short step to the conclusion that apodictic law, as a type, was also borrowed from there. This is possible, but not so certain as with the formula as a whole, since the commands and prohibitions of the treaties do not by any means show the characteristics of a type as clearly as do the series of apodictic laws in the Old Testament which are bound together by particular themes.[96] It is therefore not impossible that the forms of command and prohibition developed independently of one another in different places. Apodictic law which was already formed in Israel's nomadic prehistoric period would then, on Canaanite territory, have been fitted into the festival influenced by the Hittite treaty form.

As already indicated, it is not the purpose of what has been just said simply to deny the possibility of an extra-Israelite origin of apodictic law as a type, but rather to warn the reader against a premature certainty in the matter. Nor is it said that, if the type really did originate outside Israel, it must necessarily have been borrowed from the Hittites. For there are also commands and prohibitions in the Egyptian Wisdom literature, and it is therefore not impossible that these served the creator of the Decalogue as a model. If a connection could be shown here, then, at the same

---

[95] See B. Rothenberg, Y. Aharoni and A. Hashimshoni, *Die Wüste Gottes*, Munich and Zürich, 1961, p. 114.

[96] These themes are brought together by Alt, 'Ursprünge', p. 320.

time, a new argument would have been found for the Mosaic origin of the Decalogue.

ADDITIONS

In the last paragraph above, Stamm warns against premature certainty on the origin of apodictic law, and the wealth of work which has been done in the comparatively short time since he wrote certainly shows that he was right to make the warning. And if, at the beginning of this last section, Stamm could say in connection with Alt's fundamental work that questions still remain and that answers are being given which do not correspond to Alt's, we can now say that there are even more questions and answers. Since the work on these matters is already taking on voluminous proportions, and since it is still very much in progress, our survey now can only be somewhat sketchy and very much of a preliminary nature.[97]

On p. 36 above, Stamm raises the question of the law which the ancestors of Israel had in the period before they became members of the amphictyony of twelve tribes, and on p. 43 he mentions the possibility of the formation of Israel's apodictic law in her nomadic prehistoric period. His specific suggestion in the former connection that an answer ought to be sought from the cuneiform tablets of Mari has not yet, to the best of my knowledge, produced any definite results,[98] though this is not to say that it will not. But in this general direction, some valuable work has been done. In an article on Lev. 18, Karl Elliger finds a dodecalogue in vv. 7–17a[99] which was perhaps based on an older decalogue.[100] The prohibitions are not concerned with incest in particular but with the common life of the families within the clan, and, as far as content is concerned, the prohibitions and the reasons given for them could have originated in Israel's nomadic period and even in pre-Yahwistic times. But he still thinks that the apodictic form makes it advisable to date the prohibitions in their present form later,[101] that is, in the time when Israel, now under Yahweh's will, was already in Palestine or at least on the way there.

---

[97] See also now A. S. Kapelrud, 'Some Recent Points of View on the Time and Origin of the Decalogue', *Studia Theologica* 18, 1964, pp. 81–90.

[98] I.e. since the work of Noth mentioned on p. 36, n. 74.

[99] K. Elliger, 'Das Gesetz Leviticus 18', *ZAW* 67, 1955, pp. 1–25, here p. 7.

[100] *Ibid.*, p. 11.   [101] See below, p. 47.

In what is probably the most important work to appear on this particular subject in recent times, Erhard Gerstenberger[102] does not hesitate to date the apodictic form to the earliest times. But, first of all, it will be necessary to say something about the way in which he believes, in distinction from the views of Alt, he must now characterize the various forms in which the laws of the Old Testament appear, and the way in which they differ from one another. He thinks that it is impossible to make the distinction between casuistic and apodictic formulations in such a way that, in the latter, one is left with various sub-groups which are not identical either in form or intention.[103] None of Alt's formal criteria for apodictic clauses—metrical structure, the formation into series, formulation in the second person singular—can hold the different elements of the 'genuine Israelite law' in a unity, since they are partly of a too general nature, and partly true for only one sub-group of apodictic law. As far as the content is concerned, much, especially the participial clauses and the relative constructions, really belongs to casuistic law, because it also reckons with the transgression of a legal norm, and in a stipulation of the legal consequence, lays down a punishment for this particular case. Further, that which in a legal clause might be called the categorical is not a typical characteristic of apodictic law, for every legal clause, however it is formulated, has the intention of expressing the legal sanction categorically. It is therefore necessary that a new grouping of Old Testament legal material be undertaken. Gerstenberger speaks of 'genuine legal clauses' and these are characterized by two elements: definition of the crime, and stipulation of the legal consequence (Ex. 21.12, 15–17, for example, would be included here). But, in contrast to these, there are the prohibitions and commands which have no stipulation of the legal consequence. They have a completely different attitude; man is the hypothetical doer (he is addressed as the one who has to fashion his life in the future), and the crime is the hypothetical deed. Their purpose is to fit the life of the individual into that of the social group, and they do not look back to a crime which has been committed, as the genuine legal clauses

[102] *Wesen und Herkunft des 'apodiktischen Rechts'*, Neukirchen, 1965. See also now his article in English, 'Covenant and Commandment', *JBL* 84, 1965, pp. 38–51.
[103] *Apodiktisches Recht*, pp. 23 ff.

do, but they are a preliminary warning which does not even have the intention of forcing observance. This is the material which remains over from all that Alt called 'apodictic' law, and, as newly defined, it is an independent type. In this material we have to do mainly with prohibitions, and for these, in the material as newly defined, Gerstenberger uses the term *Prohibitive*. We shall simply use the word 'prohibitions'.

There follows a survey of the extant material[104] from the Book of the Covenant, Deuteronomy, the Holiness Code and, lastly, the Decalogues and miscellaneous material. As far as the Decalogues are concerned (Ex. 20.2 ff [Deut. 5.6 ff]; Ex. 34.12 ff), no casuistic laws whatsoever are to be found in them.

Turning to the question of the origin of apodictic law,[105] Gerstenberger notes first that the prohibitions are commonly derived from the postulated Festival of the Renewal of the Covenant, but remarks rightly that it is difficult to accommodate all apodictic clauses in one principal festival of the amphictyony. The framework, where Yahweh is the subject (e.g. Ex. 20.2), is clearly of cultic origin, but the question still remains whether the apodictic clauses themselves originated in the cult. In the Decalogue, strange to say, only the first two commandments are expressed with the 'I' of Yahweh. Even the third commandment, not to take Yahweh's name in vain, is not expressed as Yahweh's own word, and the following clauses of the series likewise mention Yahweh only in the third person. This is astonishing, since no collection of law makes so strong a claim to be the proclamation of the will of Yahweh in his own person as the Decalogue. As far as the self-introductory formula of Yahweh in v. 2 is concerned, the form-critical investigations of Elliger and Zimmerli have illuminated its cultic origin. It has the task of introducing or concluding outstanding pieces of the liturgy, and the very fact that it can be inserted at various points in the cultic celebration emphasizes its independence. Zimmerli himself comes to a similar conclusion.[106] It is possible that the self-introductory formula and the prohibition of other gods and of images formed an original unity, but it is unlikely that proclamation of command as such was always unified with it.

Gerstenberger comes to a similar conclusion on Ex. 34.12 ff

---

[104] *Apodiktisches Recht*, pp. 28 ff.   [105] *Ibid.*, pp. 55 ff.
[106] 3 'Ich bin Jahwe', *GAT*, p. 191, n. 2 = *GO*, p. 23, n. 26.

and Lev. 18 f.[107] In connection with Lev. 18, we come to what seems to me too to be the obvious, and in one way correct, comment on Elliger's views mentioned above.[108] Gerstenberger says that matters are so clear here that it is only by giving way to the traditional view that Elliger can reject what is really his own opinion, that the corpus represents an old order of the clan, and then maintain the cultic origin. As far as I can see, however, Elliger does not speak of a cultic origin of these prohibitions. What he says is about the date of their origin, and is admittedly too much conditioned by the traditional view. Gerstenberger goes on to say that, if the styling of almost all the prohibitions as the speech of Yahweh can be seen to be secondary, then it is unlikely that they originated in the Covenant Festival, and they were not always supported by Yahweh's absolute authority. Their mixture of authority and trust in a reasoned persuasion, and the way in which they desire to ensure an easily grasped order of things, leads Gerstenberger to derive their authority from a patriarchal institution, and not from the state or the priests. Even Gerstenberger's consideration of the question of the formation of the prohibitions into series[109] does not support the thesis of an origin in the Festival of the Covenant. An analysis of Lev. 19.1–18; Ex. 22.20 ff; Deut. 22–25 brings him to the conclusion that the prohibitions generally emerge in groups of one, two or three, seldom more, and the numbering of ten or twelve is foreign to them. Further, there were many practical necessities which influenced the bringing together of the maxims in their simple and series form into still larger groupings. Such matters were the instruction of youth, juridical practice, literary treatment of the material, catalogues of 'virtues', confessional formulae and prophetic rebuke. Indeed, Gerstenberger thinks that the tradition of the *ten* commandments might even be exilic! The only passages which expressly mention the ten words are Ex. 34.28; Deut. 4.13; 10.4 and, since the first is uncertain, this means that literary witness cannot be found until the time of Deuteronomy anyway. A completely undisputed numbering of ten cannot be found in any of the decalogues so this seems to confirm that this tradition

---

[107] *Apodiktisches Recht*, pp. 59 ff.
[108] P. 44. On this matter, see also G. Fohrer in the article mentioned below, p. 55, n. 129.
[109] *Op. cit.*, pp. 77 ff.

is secondary. Certainly, groupings of ten and twelve probably have their roots principally in the cult, since the tradition of ten commandments is cultic, though this late tradition does not necessarily mark the first cultic use of the prohibitions.

But this is just the point: cultic *use*. Gerstenberger points out,[110] as Mowinckel had already recognized,[111] that Alt's argumentation makes the cultic use of the prohibitions and their collections clear, but provides no satisfactory proof of cultic *origin*. In order to show that the necessary connection between the narration of the making of the covenant and the inserted collections of prohibitions cannot be proved, Gerstenberger turns to the Sinai pericope. Here, literary-critical analysis can only come to the negative result that the collections of commandments appear as insertions in the sources, and form-critical investigation can provide only a sketch of the cultic festival and not its exact content or the absolutely certain order in which the elements of this liturgy follow. And since there are many kinds of law in the Sinai tradition, the simple concept of 'promulgation of law' is not sufficient to prove the *origin* of the *apodictic* clauses. In the most ancient account of the Sinai event, Ex. 24.1–2,9–11 (E), there is certainly the implication that conduct corresponding to the covenant is expected of the partners, but it does not need to be expressed in any prescriptions, it follows of itself. Further, though the other account in Ex. 24 (vv. 3–8) does reckon with a promulgation of law, the fact that this is not given in this narrative, but that there probably exists in v. 3 a reference back to the Book of the Covenant,[112] probably means that 'words' and 'ordinances' are a later addition to this covenant narration. Gerstenberger comes to a similar conclusion for Ex. 34.10–28, and then finds in Ex. 19 f a similar division between narrative and law. The course of the narrative has been interrupted by the insertion of the Decalogue where it does not fit, between Ex. 19.19 and 20.18 ff; these passages obviously belong together, and the Decalogue itself says nothing of any making of a covenant.

This much can be established: the original texts of the Sinai *narrative* which have the making of the covenant as their theme

---

[110] *Op. cit.*, pp. 89 ff.

[111] 'Zur Geschichte der Dekaloge', *ZAW* 55, 1937, pp. 219 f.

[112] The Book of the Covenant does not belong to the original complex of the Sinai narrative and it did not originate in the cult.

have no place for the prohibitions, and, on the other hand, the great majority of these would be meaningless in an act of covenant making, since one would expect them to have to do with the relationship between the partners of the covenant. Most of them, however, are concerned with relationships between man and man and would have grown up more naturally in other circumstances. This does not mean to say that these latter ordinances were meaningless for the covenant ceremony as it came to be used, since they would have been absorbed into it in the process by which the apodictic clauses as a type were gradually drawn into the covenant formula. Here there was, of course, a crucial theological decision, namely that Yahweh was not only the sole God, but also that he rules over all spheres of life.

But Gerstenberger then has to ask whether the prohibitions could not have originated in a 'profane' covenantal ceremony, and comes to the question of the ancient oriental treaties.[113] Without denying parallels in the form and content of the prohibitions and in the construction of the covenantal formula, Gerstenberger does not, however, find the attempt of Mendenhall, Heinemann and Baltzer to find the origin of the prohibitions in the covenantal formula convincing. As a question of method, he objects that, in a form of such composite nature, it is probable that the original types would only be found in a secondary use. The following series of individual observations which preclude a form-critical identification is, however, more important:

(1) The stipulations of the vassal treaties are directed exclusively towards the conclusion of a concrete, political treaty between the suzerain and the vassal. This is even the case in those stipulations which at first sight seem to contain more general prohibitions and commands, as, for example, the demand to show confidence in the suzerain. Certainly, the Israelite prohibitions also presuppose a given social structure, but within this they claim to be universally valid and lasting. The loyalty which was also demanded for this social structure is, however, not the ruling principle of the prohibitions. The unstipulated nature of the address and of the situation expresses rather an interest in so directing the conduct of those in the fellowship that 'right' may be done as the result of every action. The attitude in the treaties which makes political

[113] *Apodiktisches Recht*, pp. 96 ff.

'right' into a function of the state is in principle different. Thus, the two are not on the same level. (2) The peculiarity of the treaty stipulations can be demonstrated by their form. They are directed to a particular man and generally lose their validity after the reign of one man. Every conditional clause seeks to define the particular situation of the vassal, and, above all, all stipulations are anchored in the particular treaty in which they occur, for they are almost regularly connected with the oaths which give them validity within the framework of the treaty. (3) But, like the conditional clauses of the treaties, the stipulations which resemble the prohibitions are also conditioned by the situation and the threat of a sanction, whereas the prohibitions are in their very nature free of sanctions. (4) A constitutive feature of the Israelite prohibitions is the tendency to be formed into series, but the treaty formula hinders this unless it takes place under the general theme of breaking the treaty.

All this taken together can only lead to the conclusion that the Old Testament prohibitions cannot be derived from the treaty formula. Gerstenberger is of the opinion that Heinemann's attempt to explain the differences[114] in the prohibitions because of their place in the cult, their oral transmission and their rhythmic form is not convincing.

Gerstenberger now turns in detail to his thesis that the origin of the prohibitions is to be found in the Semitic clan-association, and that they were the authoritative commandments of the elders of the clan or the family, though they do not receive their authority so much from the individual power of these figures as from the sanctified order which they represent.[115]

He refers to the story in Jer. 35 of the loyalty of the Rechabites to their tradition, where the prohibition against drinking wine is quoted as a valid norm. There is, however, in addition to this a series of prohibitions which is actually not relevant to the matter in hand. The author of these words is the clan father, Jonadab, who stands as the highest authority in his clan and whose prescriptions are called a 'command' (*miṣwā* in the singular) which appears to be almost a technical term. The prohibitions are not timeless maxims, but localized formations for the special situation of this clan. The capacity to create law thus belongs to the clan

---

[114] *Untersuchungen zum apodiktischen Recht*, § 17.
[115] *Op. cit.*, pp. 110 ff.

father who is the author of those ordinances which hold together the fellowship subject to him. It may be that this Rechabite commandment was an exclusive matter to which there are no parallels, but it is incontestable that such ordinances were handed on in the clan. Another text is Lev. 18 which has already been discussed in connection with Elliger's article on this chapter.[116] Here also we have to do with the community life of the clan.

The themes of the prohibitions which Gerstenberger had already outlined[117] correspond for the most part with the interests of the clan. Seeing their general theme was the ordering of daily life which was not confined to the profane, the number of prohibitions which have to do with the cult is surprisingly great. But their chief concern does not lie here, but with actions towards people and things in which questions concerning the ties of blood or society are involved. Such themes are: murder, theft, capital crimes, sex, conduct in the law-court, lack of consideration for the lower social classes, swindling, lying, false oath, disregard for the inviolability of property and lack of consideration for animals. Further, the frequent mention of the brother, the people, the neighbour (the native), along with the exclusion of the foreigner and the special mention of the stranger, show the intimate connection of the prohibitions with the blood relationship of the clan. Their whole social, economic and formal structure corresponds to the life of the Hebrew clan even if there are no direct references in the prohibitions themselves to their assumed origin. Here, the father was the person of authority though he also lived under the laws for the ordering of the family which stood under the protection of God.[118] The prohibitions were certainly also entrusted to the young man who was growing into the authority of a family head.

Gerstenberger then seeks to confirm his thesis by a study of the Wisdom literature. Parts of this show a clan background which is similar to that of the prohibitions, and thematically, they also provide many parallel exhortations and warnings, and proverbs dealing with the very matters which were included in the list of prohibitions above. It is true that there are very few prohibitions of violence, but sexual, social and legal conduct are favourite

[116] In *ZAW* 67, 1955, pp. 1–25; see above, p. 44.
[117] *Apodiktisches Recht*, pp. 61 ff.
[118] See Gen. 38.26; Judg. 11.30 f, 35 ff.

themes. Gerstenberger distinguishes between two main types in Wisdom literature:[119] the 'instructions' (*Weisungen*) formulated in direct address, and the 'sentences' (*Sentenzen*) in impersonal style.[120] Since the various collections of proverbs within the Book of Proverbs as a whole contain, to a large degree, only one of these types, the two could have different origins. For the first, he postulates the situation of the instruction of the father of the family, and the oral instruction which is expressly mentioned in the later collections of Wisdom confirms this. In an analysis of Prov. 22–24, he finds, within the 'instructions', warning and exhortatory words for which reasons are given by a subsidiary clause. But the variety of grammatical and stylistic forms in the latter, as well as other factors, suggest that the warning word was originally independent. The aim of this instruction by the father is not only 'character formation', but also to prevent particular failures in social contact. The sphere of application of the warning words is conditioned by the intimate relationships of the clan; they have the purpose of regulating the relationships with such groups of people as father and mother, the minor, the poor, the fools and the evil. Further, they are on a completely private level; there are no signs of an 'official' cultic or political institution. The king and those in power are only mentioned by chance, and Yahweh and the cult play no part at all.

Thus, the analogy with the legal prohibitions cannot be denied, and it is not only that a number of these exhortatory and warning words correspond with them in content—this has been frequently observed and never satisfactorily explained—but the decisive thing is that analysis results in the same or at least in a similar point of origin. This is not to deny that there are differences and that the type has developed further in the Wisdom tradition.

Gerstenberger then turns to a consideration of parallels in the Wisdom literature of the Ancient Near East.[121] There is hardly anything from the Sumerian fragments which is comparable to the prohibitions, but there is some material from Babylonian–Assyrian territory—it all falls under the category of confession or omens—which reminds us of the warning words and prohibitions, and corresponding prohibitions can be won from the present omen

[119] *Op. cit.*, pp. 117 ff.   [120] Cf. Prov. 22.22 with 14.31.
[121] *Op. cit.*, pp. 130 ff.

form. From Egypt, direct witnesses are available for the existence of collections of prohibitions and commandments in the various royal instructions—the best known is that of Amen-em-Opet. In all these parallel texts, the negative formulation plays an important part, as a glance at the Instruction of Amen-em-Opet is sufficient to show.[122] Since, in most cases, the prohibitions introduce the section, and it is only as a second part that general exhortations follow, it can also be said that the formulation in Wisdom style is secondary. Gerstenberger comes to the conclusion that there was an ancient Near Eastern class of rules formulated predominantly in the negative (second person singular) which was preserved in various literary types, and that its original form completely corresponds with that of the Old Testament prohibitions. There is also correspondence in content which, since it has to do with a *Volksethos*, already tells us something about the origin of the form. The natural division of ancient Near Eastern peoples was according to family and clan, and the intimate address in the second person singular, as well as the occasional picture of the inexperienced young person being instructed by fatherly authority, make an origin from the clan likely. We would thus have to reckon with an international spread of a clan ethos expressed in prohibitions which not only held together the most stable social group, but which also set up everywhere similar laws for human conduct together. This old clan order must still have represented the universal norm for good and evil even though it had its origin in small social units.

In the last section to concern us here, Gerstenberger considers the question of the development of the form from its origin in the clan to its use in the cult on the one hand, and to its reception into the Wisdom literature on the other.[123] When the Israelites began to lead a settled life, they came into contact with the much more highly developed legal culture of the Canaanites. As they adapted themselves in Palestine, this casuistic system was necessarily the one which was more useful in their 'justice in the gate', though the oral tradition of the clan may also have been taken up supplementarily into the written corpora. But it is not only Canaanite influence which is relevant. There was a far-reaching social reformation of the ancient clan order itself; the civic community becomes more important than the blood relationship of the clan, and is then

[122] *ANET*, pp. 421b ff.   [123] *Apodiktisches Recht*, pp. 141 ff.

in its turn replaced by the monarchical order of the state. As far as the cult is concerned, the order of the clan had stood under divine protection since ancient times, and thus some relation of the prohibitions to the cult must be very old. Penitential ceremonies and purification oaths, etc., demanded a confession of guilt or an adjuration of innocence, and once the prohibitions in the form of confessions came into contact with the cult, the occasion was given for their collection. Entry Liturgies probably originated in this way, as did the collections of commandments and prohibitions which, like the Decalogue, were used in the cult as a proclamation of the will of the divinity. The historical narrative of the Sinai revelation would not have been added until later—a feature which seems to have no parallel in the ancient Near East. Finally, a class of the 'wise' had long existed in ancient oriental society, and the exhortations and warnings of the clan ethos came into their hands as well.

This summary of the work of Gerstenberger shows how different his views are, not only from those of Alt, but also from those of more recent scholars like Mendenhall, Heinemann and Baltzer. It is interesting that Hans Jochen Boecker[124] has now also disputed the cultic origin of that type of law which Gerstenberger calls 'genuine legal clauses', and which he maintains is not true apodictic law. In his chapter on the forms of speech at the conclusion of a trial, Boecker considers the consequences which result from the conviction, and calls this the stipulation of the consequence of the deed (*Tatfolgebestimmung*). These are now to be found among the Old Testament laws. In framing the stipulations, the court of law could have made use of laws already existent, but, on the other hand, the laws which we now have could have developed from the stipulations which originated in the judicial process itself. Boecker thinks that the latter was primarily the case since, to quote a sentence from Alt, 'the formation of law is fundamentally a procedure not of literary creation, but of life as it is lived', and also because it can be seen from Num. 15.32 ff or I Sam. 30.24 f, for instance, how a law can develop from a case of precedent.[125] One of the best-known stipulations of the con-

---

[124] *Redeformen des Rechtslebens im Alten Testament*, Neukirchen, 1964, pp. 143 ff.
[125] The quotation from Alt is from 'Ursprünge', *KS* I, p. 284. Boecker also refers to Gerstenberger (a note omitted from his book, but in the Dissertation [Bonn, 1961] on which it is based, p. 133, n. 22).

sequence of the deed is the formula 'he shall surely die' (*mōt yūmāt*), though, since Alt connected this with 'apodictic' law,[126] and this in turn meant that it could have nothing to do with 'profane' legal practice, its character as a stipulation of the consequence has often not been recognized; it has been described as a 'curse formula'.[127] In Boecker's opinion, however, Gerstenberger's work has cleared these difficulties out of the way (if he is right the formula will belong to casuistic law anyway), and there is nothing to stop it being understood as a stipulation of the consequence of the deed, and as originating in 'profane' law. This is shown by the fact that in Gen. 26.11 and Ex. 19.12b it stands in a context which clearly shows legal styling, and there are also a number of other short, similarly constructed stipulations of the consequence of the deed which confirm that 'he shall surely die' was also rooted in the sphere of normal jurisdiction, and was not a curse formula of sacral law.

Earlier in his book,[128] Boecker has noted that, while modifications must now be made to Alt's conception of 'apodictic' law, there is still a good deal to be said for seeing it, in its present form, in connection with the amphictyony, even though differences in formulation and origin can be seen within it.

The work of George Fohrer on this subject[129] shows at least some similarities to that of Gerstenberger. Fohrer sees the origin of the apodictically formulated series among nomads or semi-nomads, and himself summarizes his views as follows: (1) A distinction has to be made between apodictic *style* (in which both individual clauses and series could be formulated) and apodictic *series* which consist of several identically formulated clauses. (2) Apodictic style—'do this' or 'do not do that'—is as old as the first command or prohibition formed by human beings and belongs to the primitive forms of human speech; there is thus no point is seeking

---

[126] *KS* I, pp. 278 ff.

[127] E.g. by Reventlow, ' "Sein Blut komme über sein Haupt" ', *VT* 10, 1960, pp. 316 f; *Das Heiligkeitsgesetz*, Neukirchen, 1961, pp. 38 and 80 ff. On Reventlow's criticism of Boecker and Gerstenberger, see below, pp. 58 ff. [128] *Op. cit.*, p. 19, n. 1.

[129] 'Das sogenannte apodiktisch formulierte Recht und der Dekalog', *Kerygma und Dogma* 11, 1965, pp. 49–74. I thank Professor Fohrer for kindly allowing me to see a copy of his work before publication. There is a good deal else in this article which I might have mentioned in other parts of this book, but as the latter was almost complete before I was able to see Fohrer's work, I have not done so.

a common origin in the various ancient Near Eastern literatures. (3) It is likely that the formation of series took place in the nomadic or semi-nomadic sphere since, in illiterate circles, such a formation with ten or twelve clauses was a help for memorizing. (4) There is not only one genre in apodictic style, but several. Command and prohibition alone form two of them, and others were added in the course of time. (5) The series of apodictically formulated clauses do not always contain 'law'. They can simply be a norm of conduct which commands or recommends a particular deed (or its omission) without any legal sanction; it is only in the Book of the Covenant that corresponding legal stipulations can be found.

The reason for finding the origin of the apodictic series among the nomads or semi-nomads becomes apparent if we consider Lev. 18 (an original decalogue). This means that they are not 'genuinely Israelite' and Yahwistic, and that the relationship with Yahweh and the proclamation as law does not stand at the beginning of the development, but at its end. As far as the Decalogue is concerned, Fohrer does not think that it was an original series of identically formulated apodictic clauses like Lev. 18, but that it was secondarily constructed. This explains the existence of three different kinds of apodictic formulation in Ex. 20.3–17, and it is thus most likely that the Decalogue clauses are taken from three different apodictic series. Five prohibitions (I–III and IX–X) come from a series with four stresses, three (VI–VIII) from a series with two stresses (see Hos. 4.2; Jer. 7.9), and two commandments (IV–V) from a series with three stresses. As far as the age and origin of the Decalogue clauses are concerned, Fohrer thinks it clear that I–III presuppose faith in Yahweh, though exact dating is not possible. Nothing stands in the way of their coming from the time of Moses, but it cannot be proved. If they were common to all Israel, as their use in Ex. 20 (to be attributed to E, according to Fohrer) and Ex. 34 suggests, then they must have originated long before the division of the kingdom after the death of Solomon. The same could no doubt be said for IX–X, but there are no indications of the age and origin of the prohibitions and commandments in the other two series. They could be derived just as well from nomadic, pre-Yahwistic times as from Palestinian, Yahwistic times, though the comparatively short time of the wandering of the group led by Moses can hardly be considered as the time of origin for several groups of apodictic series.

The question when the Decalogue as we now have it was first put together cannot be answered with certainty either. It seems most probable that it was done by E. But the fact that it is a secondary formation makes it extremely doubtful that its origin was in the cult; it was designed rather as a rule for life and conduct.

The similarity between Gerstenberger and Fohrer consists in the fact that both see a relationship between apodictic law and the clan ethos or nomadic times. But even here there are differences in detail; Gerstenberger finds the origin of the apodictic clauses themselves in the clan ethos, whereas Fohrer allows this only for the series, in nomadic times, and speaks of a general origin of apodictic law itself. This does not seem to me to be very helpful in the Old Testament context, because here we have to do with prohibitions like 'you shall not kill' which have a certain content stemming from a particular order, and, in nomadic times, we cannot be too far away from the time when such a content arose. It is doubtful whether there is any point in calling such a clause as 'do not kill that dinosaur' apodictic law. Another difference is that Gerstenberger sees the series of ten as late, and as originating in the cult, whereas Fohrer finds a series of ten in nomadic times in Lev. 18, and, as far as the Decalogue is concerned, denies the cultic origin of this series of ten.

The most important difference between the two, as far as we are concerned, is that Fohrer is much more cautious about an early dating than Gerstenberger is. It is true that Gerstenberger was not primarily concerned with applying insights into the origin of apodictic law to the origin of the Decalogue clauses in particular, but, when comparing the prohibitions with the 'instructions', he has said enough about their similarity in theme and circumstances of origin to make it likely that at least some of them originated in the early clan ethos.[130] Fohrer makes no reference to this. He has taken a step in the right direction in applying this whole discussion to the Decalogue clauses themselves, but questions still remain. Could I–III have had their origin in the cult?[131] Can IX–X simply be taken together with I–III? Will it perhaps be possible, through investigations along the lines of Gerstenberger's in texts relating

[130] See above, pp. 51 f. Thematic comparisons can, at the very least, be made between Prov. 23.22 and Ex. 20.12; Prov. 24.28 and Ex. 20.16; Prov. 24.15 and Ex. 20.17; see Gerstenberger, *Apodiktisches Recht*, p. 129.
[131] On the origin of the first commandment, see also now Rolf Knierim, 'Das erste Gebot', *ZAW* 77, 1965, pp. 20–39.

to the clan ethos, to come to an even more definite conclusion concerning the origin of the individual Decalogue clauses themselves than Gerstenberger has already indicated and than Fohrer thinks is possible?

Fohrer seems to have implied criticisms of Gerstenberger; others, however, have made direct criticisms of both Gerstenberger and Boecker.[132] Horst Seebass,[133] in noting that the Decalogue which follows Ex. 20.1 certainly cannot be linked with any of the ancient sources since it shows relationships with the P tradition, thinks that the easiest solution is to be found in postulating that this Decalogue has replaced an earlier one—that is, that the earlier sources too expounded the Sinai revelation in the form of a decalogue. Noting the changes in attitude to the Decalogue in Gerstenberger's work, he says that if the latter's thesis[134] that the name of Yahweh was directly connected with cultic commandments is right, then the Sinai legislation, which in his opinion cannot be eliminated entirely,[135] was perhaps more related to the Aaronite legislation than was allowed for in this work. Later,[136] Seebass says that, since it has been shown that at least some of the formulations of law in the decalogue-like series go back to the earliest times, it can be postulated that the starting-point for the development of divine law, in as far as it is brought into connection with Sinai, was a decalogue form. The Sinai tradition in its origin is the starting-point for the understanding of the Mosaic features, and Moses cannot be separated from Sinai.

None of this takes account of Gerstenberger's arguments for the late origin of the Ten Commandments as a series,[137] but it should not be overlooked that it is not Seebass's purpose to attempt a detailed criticism of Gerstenberger. This has, however, been attempted by Reventlow.[138] He does not dispute the im-

---

[132] For views different to Gerstenberger's, see also now W. Beyerlin, 'Die Paränese im Bundesbuch und ihre Herkunft', *Gottes Wort und Gottes Land, Hans-Wilhelm Hertzberg zum 70. Geburtstag*, ed. by H. Reventlow, Göttingen, 1965, pp. 9–29.

[133] H. Seebass, *Mose und Aaron, Sinai und Gottesberg*, Bonn, 1962, pp. 113 f.

[134] *Apodiktisches Recht*, p. 59; see above p. 46.

[135] Against Gerstenberger, *ibid.*, pp. 92 f; see above, pp. 48 f.

[136] *Op. cit.*, pp. 118 f.

[137] See above, pp. 47 f—though cf. Fohrer, art. cit., *Kerygma und Dogma* 11, pp. 66 ff; see also below, p. 69.

[138] H. Reventlow, 'Kultisches Recht im Alten Testament', *ZThK* 60, 1963, pp. 267–304.

portance of Gerstenberger's work,[139] and he does not wish to
support the thesis that Israel was directly dependent on the
Hittite vassal treaties.[140] But the thesis that only some prohibitions
have an original connection with the cult, whereas others are
grounded in relationships within the clan, does not seem to him
to be satisfactory since they are still rooted in a sacral sphere, as he
says Gerstenberger himself 'admits'.[141] He goes on to ask whether
the placing of the origin of the prohibitions in the clan ethos or in
the cult of the Covenant Festival is really an either-or. Here
again he places weight on the fact that Gerstenberger himself
stresses that the order of the clan is laid down by the divinity
himself. But saying that the prohibitions originated in the clan
ethos which was regarded as an order stemming from the divinity
is not the same as saying that they had their origin in a cultic
procedure.

Then Reventlow criticizes Gerstenberger's comparison of the
prohibitions with the hortatory and warning words of the
Wisdom literature[142] by saying that the obvious parallels in form
and content are overrated, and that the assumption of identical
origin is hardly convincing in the light of the admitted differences
in milieu and attitude. This criticism does not seem to me to do
justice to the description of the circles of people among which
both are to be found,[143] or to take account of the fact that the
circles of people will have developed differently within the
Wisdom tradition.

Reventlow then asks[144] whether a distinction between apodictic
law and casuistic law is possible at all; he does not think that
a fundamentally different point of origin can be substantiated, and
refers to the work of Stanley Gevirtz[145] on West-Semitic curse
inscriptions in which both forms occur side by side. May this not
be evidence that both forms derive from a closely related origin?
Some remarks of Rudolf Kilian[146] are also relevant here. He does
not mention a related origin, but he does not think that the first
appearance of casuistic law in Israel is necessarily as late as the

[139] *Op. cit.*, pp. 274 f.   [140] *Ibid.*, pp. 276 ff.   [141] *Ibid.*, pp. 278 ff.
[142] *Ibid.*, p. 281.   [143] See above, pp. 51 f.
[144] 'Kultisches Recht . . .', *ZThK* 60, 1963, pp. 281 ff.
[145] 'West-Semitic Curses and the Problem of the Origins of Hebrew Law',
VT 11, 1961, pp. 137–158.
[146] R. Kilian, *Literarkritische und formgeschichtliche Untersuchung des Heiligkeits-gesetzes*, Bonn, 1963, pp. 2 f.

time of the Conquest and the formation of the state. The Israelite
tribes needed a secular law before this which could be used in
ordinary legal processes, and apodictic law, even from the point
of view of content, was not sufficient for these. References to
such a law can be found, however, in the ancient narratives
of the patriarchal period, and the patriarchs were in contact
with their settled neighbours who possessed a casuistic law. However, as it seems to me, the conclusion that the ancestors of the
Israelites knew a casuistic law before the Conquest is more likely
than that it originated among them. For this, it would be necessary to prove that they did not receive it from their settled neighbours, or else that they had not themselves become at least half
settled by then. The fact that the two types exist side by side in
the West-Semitic curses does not necessarily mean that they had
the same origin. The question is: would the presuppositions for
the formation of a casuistic law have existed in a purely nomadic
community?

Reventlow goes on to ask what legal institutions could have
lain behind such a combination of apodictic and casuistic legislation.[147] He really just assumes that apodictic law is cultically
proclaimed law which came to expression in the Israelite Covenant
Festival. For him the spokesman is the prophet,[148] and he refers to
Ernst Würthwein's article[149] in which the origin of the prophetic
oracle of judgement is seen in the cult. Reventlow does not wish to
accept all the details of this, and he agrees with some of the
criticisms which have been made by Boecker[150] and others. He
thinks that Boecker is right in seeing the origin of the legal
procedure with its accusation and defence, and the hearing of
witnesses, etc., in the secular sphere of local jurisdiction, but his
conclusion that there is no cultic law whatsoever in Israel is to be
rejected. Reventlow sees the two spheres of law merging together
in the course of a centuries-long development, so that they
resulted in a combined phenomenon, the external form of which
was more or less conditioned by casuistic law, the inner content,

[147] *Op. cit.*, pp. 283 ff.

[148] See above, p. 37, n. 79.

[149] 'Der Ursprung der prophetischen Gerichtsrede', *ZThK* 49, 1952, pp.
1–16.

[150] Reventlow's references are to Boecker's dissertation (*Redeformen des
israelitischen Rechtlebens*, Diss., Bonn, 1959). In the considerably modified book
published in 1964, this discussion appears on pp. 91 ff.

however, ever more strongly by the religious statements of the amphictyonic cultic law.

But all this is puzzling because, firstly, it seems to me that it is Reventlow who comes to the conclusion that Boecker's work means that there is no such thing as cultic law at all, and not Boecker himself.[151] Indeed, Boecker's note referred to above[152] would indicate the opposite. Secondly, Reventlow himself refers to a 'centuries-long development' which must mean that other circumstances than the ones he assumes were once possible.

It must be said that there is much in this article of Reventlow's which has not been referred to, but the result does not seem to me to be very convincing. This is particularly because he does not distinguish clearly enough either between law which has a sacral framework and that which originated in the cult, or between the state of affairs as we now have it and what may once have been. Gerstenberger and Boecker have made noteworthy attempts to elucidate these very distinctions.

Reventlow's mention of Gevirtz's article can bring us now to a further consideration of apodictic law and ancient Near Eastern parallels. Stamm says[153] that if the type did originate outside Israel, it need not necessarily have been borrowed from the Hittites, and refers to Egyptian Wisdom literature. Parallels have in fact been found in various spheres. Gevirtz finds prohibitions of the same order as the apodictically formulated prohibitions of the Old Testament in West-Semitic curses, and he concludes that the uniqueness, if not the originality, in Israel of the apodictic legal style can no longer be upheld.[154] Dennis J. McCarthy[155] finds the most noteworthy example of the formulation using the second person singular imperative in the Hittite treaty of Mursilis II with Manapa-Dattas,[156] though he also finds that apodictic formulae are rare in texts written in Accadian and representing alliances with Assyrian states. He thinks that the usage may be due to a certain intimacy between the partners—a factor which would tally with Gerstenberger's postulated origin in the ethos of the clan.

---

[151] See Reventlow, *op. cit.*, cf. p. 285 with p. 297.
[152] P. 55.   [153] See above, pp. 43 f.
[154] 'West-Semitic Curses . . .', *VT* 11, 1961, p. 156.
[155] *Treaty and Covenant. A Study in Form in the Ancient Oriental Documents and in the Old Testament*, Rome, 1963, pp. 35 ff.
[156] See also the Aramaic text from Sfiré and the Assyrian treaty with Baal of Tyre; *ibid.*, p. 81.

But as far as possible contact with the Hebrew Decalogue is concerned, it has to be remembered that the Hittite treaties with the Syrians scarcely show the form, and it would have been in the Syrian part of the Hittite Empire that any contact between Hatti and Israel would have taken place. The conclusion from this evidence would seem to be that a direct dependence of Israel on the Hittites is not likely. This is borne out by the fact that the sequence of apodictically formulated commandments in the treaties is not on the same level as the series in the Decalogue. They are simply repetitions.[157]

In connection with Stamm's suggestion, Kilian does find parallels in Egyptian literature.[158] They are in the execration texts of the Eleventh Dynasty, in the tomb inscriptions of Siut, and in the decalogues in the time of Ramses II, as well as in other texts. He also has a summary of the position concerning apodictic law in the first chapter of his book on the Holiness Code,[159] as does von Rad in the introduction to his commentary on Deuteronomy.[160] Here it is interesting to note that he too thinks that Gerstenberger has demonstrated the likelihood of apodictic law having originated in the clan ethos.

All these parallels from different parts of the ancient Near Eastern world seem to make it conclusive that it is now no longer possible to speak of apodictic law as 'genuine Israelite law', at least as far as the *form* is concerned. It must, however, be noted immediately that this does not exhaust the discussion, for Gerstenberger's work in particular has made it questionable whether there was any direct dependence, and he has also drawn attention to differences in the whole *intent*.

More work has also been done on the ancient Near Eastern treaty form and the Israelite Festival of the Renewal of the Covenant.[161] F. Charles Fensham[162] speaks of a close connection in form; he is chiefly concerned with malediction and benediction.

---

[157] *Treaty and Covenant*, p. 159. Similarly Gerstenberger; see above, pp. 49 f.

[158] 'Apodiktisches und kasuistisches Recht im Licht ägyptischer Analogien', *BZ*, NS 7, 1963, pp. 185 ff.

[159] See above, p. 59, n. 146.

[160] G. von Rad, *Deuteronomy* (OTL), ETr., 1966, pp. 17 ff.

[161] See also now J. A. Thompson, *The Ancient Near Eastern Treaties and the Old Testament*, London, 1964.

[162] 'Malediction and Benediction in the Ancient Near Eastern Vassal-Treaties and the Old Testament', *ZAW* 74, 1962, pp. 1–9.

Norbert Lohfink[163] seeks to define more precisely another corresponding element, the Declaration of Basic Principle (*Grundsatzerklärung*), which, for the Old Testament, he finds in Deut. 5–11. Meredith G. Kline[164] sees a remarkable resemblance between the two; he understands the two tables (Deut. 4.13) as duplicate copies of the covenant, one for depositing in a sanctuary of the vassal and the other in a sanctuary of the suzerain (Suppiluliuma with Mattiwaza). But he wishes to use this correspondence for an early dating of Deuteronomy which, as we shall see, is very dubious.[165] Buis and Leclercq[166] see the borrowings as most evident in the benedictions and maledictions, though they think that the dependence of the Decalogue on the treaty texts is limited to the plan and some expressions. Later,[167] they see theological differences. It is not intended to say that those mentioned above, who are all more or less positive towards some kind of relation between the treaties and the covenant, do not also see differences of this latter sort.

The most detailed consideration of this topic presented recently is the work by McCarthy which we have just mentioned. He begins with a criticism of Mendenhall and Baltzer[168] and finds, against the former, that the form of the story of Sinai is not unequivocally that of the treaties. He makes some methodological criticisms, mainly that it is only on the assumption that all covenants must reflect the treaty form that one can proceed from the verification of the fact of a covenant to *the* covenant form. With regard to Baltzer, he questions whether all the instances which he gives are in fact evidence for the covenant form. He then gives a survey of the ancient Near Eastern material, starting with the earliest pre-Hittite examples,[169] and proceeding to Hittite parity and vassal treaties.[170] Here he comes to the conclusion that there was a variety within a general uniformity, though the uniformity was not absolute and the form was not rigid. The fact that the section devoted to history could be omitted is especially important. The matters never omitted were the obligations to be

[163] N. Lohfink, *Das Hauptgebot. Eine Untersuchung literarischer Einleitungsfragen zu Dtn 5–11*, Rome, 1963, e.g. p. 111.
[164] M. G. Kline, *Treaty of the Great King. The Covenant Structure of Deuteronomy*, Grand Rapids, 1963, pp. 17 ff.
[165] See below, pp. 64 f.   [166] *Le Deutéronome*, pp. 8 f.
[167] *Ibid.*, p. 73.   [168] *Treaty and Covenant*, pp. 5 ff.
[169] *Ibid.*, pp. 15 ff.   [170] *Ibid.*, pp. 22 ff.

assumed and the invocation of the gods with the consequent implication of divine sanctions. Then come treaties from Syria.[171] Here the Abba-AN treaty contains history—the only one outside the texts from Hatti which does—but this is hardly due to Hittite influence. The Sfiré text, though mutilated, clearly has elements from the treaty tradition, and there is no doubt that it belongs in the stream of the ancient Near Eastern treaty tradition. Next comes an account of the treaties from Assyria,[172] and, as with the Hittites, the elements are constant; the stipulations, the invocation of the gods, and the curses always appear. But, here too, the arrangement could have a certain freedom. The first section of the book ends with two chapters of conclusions[173] in which the author finds, firstly, that there is a fundamental unity in all the treaties, and that there is more behind this than a common origin, namely a common place and function in the social structure. But, secondly, there is a diversity: history is confined to the Hittite treaties, and a great emphasis on the curses and the use of substitution rites characterizes the treaties from Assyria and Syria. As far as the history in the case of the Hittites is concerned, it is not characteristic of the treaty in the sense that only treaties have it. It is something typically Hittite, and royal documents of every sort contain it as a kind of cautionary tale to warn and edify; it is an example, no more. The final conclusion is that even though two sub-groups occur in the treaty family—the Hittite of the second millennium with its historical section, and the Syrian–Assyrian of the first millennium with its curses and substitution rites—it is possible that the fact that the two belong to different epochs is due to a lacuna in our evidence, and we know that traditions from the older time reappear later. In view of many points of continuity between first and second millennia, it would be dangerous to come to the conclusion that there was a total break between the two sets of treaties and then to try to use this break as a criterion of date.

Fohrer remarks in his summary of the book[174] that this conclusion is of decisive importance for the Old Testament, especially as the correspondence which has been said to exist between the treaties and the Old Testament texts has been used for a conservative dating of the latter.[175] In his second section McCarthy turns to

[171] *Treaty and Covenant*, pp. 51 ff.   [172] *Ibid.*, pp. 68 ff.
[173] *Ibid.*, pp. 80 ff.   [174] *ZAW* 76, 1964, p. 236.
[175] E.g. by Kline; see above, p. 63, and below, p. 65.

the Old Testament, starting with a consideration of Deuterono-my,[176] then going on to Samuel and Joshua,[177] and concluding with Sinai.[178] In the first, he finds the treaty form:[179] the historical pro-logue, the laws, the notice that the contract has been pledged, and the blessings and curses. He finds that I Sam. 12 and Josh. 24 are on the same plane as the deuteronomic texts, but with Sinai it is different. McCarthy does not think that the Decalogue by itself is a covenant form. It only has the prologue and the ten command-ments, and, as we have already remarked,[180] he does not think that the sequence of commands in the treaties is on the same level as the series here. In the case of the prologue, even if it is not secondary (and there are reasons for thinking that it is), it is not necessarily a historical prologue in the strict sense found in the Hittite treaty, where the intention of the history is that of per-suasion, not of defining who the king is. In the Decalogue, on the other hand, the reference to historical events serves to designate the speaker, in fact continues the theophany. Then, when Ex. 24 is added, we have the sequence: coming of Yahweh, proclamation of his will, and rites by which the alliance is ratified. The ratification of alliance by rite rather than by contract based on oath, and the gesture of superior to inferior rather than *vice versa*, are not parallels to the treaty tradition. Even other elements in Ex. 24 which recall aspects of the treaties are not completely true parallels. McCarthy also concludes that the form of the Sinai story in Ex. 19–24 which is reflected in the text without later additions does not confirm that it reflects an organization according to the covenant form, as in Deuteronomy. Ritual plays a greater part than the verbal and contractual. The overall con-clusion is that, contrary to the normal process where the form is usually at its clearest and most rigid in early examples, here the form reaches its full development in Deuteronomy, that is at the end and not at the beginning of the development.

This means that neither an early dating of the covenant form nor any sort of direct dependence on extra-Israelite forms can be inferred, since the earliest situation in the Old Testament in which it could be expected does not show dependence. Thus, even

---

[176] *Op. cit.*, pp. 109 ff.   [177] *Ibid.*, pp. 141 ff.   [178] *Ibid.*, pp. 152 ff.
[179] Though even this can be put into doubt; see Gerstenberger's review of the book, *JBL* 83, 1964, pp. 198 f.
[180] See above, p. 62.

though McCarthy does not seem to have known Gerstenberger's work when he wrote his book, he comes to a similar conclusion, at least as far as the Sinai pericope is concerned. The work of both scholars has the effect of separating off the commands/prohibitions in their original setting into an earlier, independent sphere.

There are also other writers who doubt whether the Old Testament covenantal form is directly dependent on the ancient Near Eastern treaty form. A remark of Rudolf Smend[181] can be interpreted as putting the directness of this connection into question. He says that, as far as he can see, Baltzer does not quote any parallels from the Hittite treaties to the 'covenantal summary'[182] which would certainly have been an important element of a covenantal formula which might once have existed. James Barr[183] goes further. He thinks that Mendenhall's attempt to invoke the similarities to the Hittite treaties only picks out points which might belong to any treaty supported by sacral sanctions, and that it does not explain more for the covenant in Israel than at most the form of certain developed statements of it. It seems to him in any case that a tradition of a covenant with Abraham is old, and not merely a secondary extension back of the Mosaic covenant.

One of the difficulties here is that we can no longer be very sure about the construction and scope of the Israelite Covenant Festival itself! We have already mentioned[184] that Gerstenberger thinks it difficult to accommodate all apodictic clauses in one principal festival of the amphictyony. In my opinion, this should have been said a long time ago,[185] but it does not necessarily mean that there was no such festival or that no apodictic law played a part in it. Baltzer[186] questions whether there was a regular renewal of the covenant and thinks of a reading rather than a ritual, and Smend[187] says that it is difficult to think of an act which was celebrated regularly, let alone annually. We are not going to go in detail into this complicated question here. Suffice it to say that some kind of an act is not being denied altogether and to refer

[181] *Die Bundesformel*, Zürich, 1963, p. 34, n. 16.
[182] *Bundesformel* not *Bundesformular*, i.e. 'I shall be your God, and you shall be my people'.
[183] Article 'Covenant', *HDB*, p. 184a.
[184] See above, p. 46.
[185] It should be noted too that a good deal of other material has also been attributed to this festival.
[186] *Das Bundesformular*, 2nd ed., Neukirchen, 1964, pp. 48 ff and 91 ff.
[187] *Op. cit.*, pp. 8 f.

back to the evidence which has been brought forward concerning the construction of the festival and the part which the Decalogue clauses played in it.[188] One cannot, however, be blind to the difficulty that the evidence is pieced together in fragments, and that the exact nature, elements, sequence and frequency of this act are still very much open to discussion. Von Rad[189] says that it is not to be wondered at that the covenantal formula in the Old Testament cannot be made out in its entirety, since its transference from the political sphere to the relationship of Yahweh with Israel made certain modifications necessary, and he adds that the question how Israel came to understand this relationship in the form of ancient Near Eastern vassal treaties is still wide open. To which one might add, in the light of the discussion above, that the questions whether the difficulty can be seen in just this way, and whether there is any direct dependence at all are also still open.

After all this detail, it might be wondered whether it is possible to come to any conclusions at all. It must certainly be stressed that the discussion is still very much in progress, and that whatever is said now will be of a preliminary nature and that it runs the risk of being one-sided. However, with these reservations, the following is offered for consideration.

With regard to Alt's definition of apodictic law, it seems clear that it is now necessary to make distinctions within this. The participial constructions with their stipulation of the consequence of the deed do, in fact, seem to be more like casuistic law than like the negative constructions in the second person singular which express no consequence at all. At the same time, however, it must be said that the questions of the differences which may exist between these participial constructions and casuistic law as Alt understood it and apodictic law as newly defined still remain open.

It also seems clear that we can no longer speak of apodictic law as 'genuine Israelite law', meaning that it exists only there. This is made impossible by the clear parallels which exist in many parts of the ancient Near Eastern world, at least in *form*. It must certainly be considered that there are differences in *intent*, and this is likely to form an important part of the discussion in the future. Also, it seems probable that the existent parallels are not the result of

---

[188] See above, pp. 28 ff and 37 ff.   [189] *Deuteronomy*, pp. 21 f.

direct dependence, but of a common tradition—most likely that of the clan.

Following on from this, it seems to me that the most convincing explanation as yet of the origin of apodictic law is to be found in Gerstenberger's thesis of the origin in the clan, because it is the one which deals most satisfactorily with all the questions which arise. His work does not necessarily mean that all the clauses of the *Decalogue* had this origin, but he has provided enough material, especially in his consideration of the themes of the prohibitions, to make this the most likely thing for at least some of them. As we have seen, Gerstenberger's opinions have not gone unchallenged, but I think that it is at least true to say that the main discussion in the near future will centre around his work.

Thus the origin of apodictic law is not in the cult or in the treaties. This does not mean to say that it did not come to be expressed in the cult in a form which had at least some relationship with the treaties. To have drawn attention to this is the merit of the work of Mendenhall and Baltzer in particular. But this relationship was not necessarily one of direct dependence. McCarthy has pointed out the difficulty of defining a point of contact where at the same time a treaty form existed which is closely enough parallel to what we have in the Old Testament. This does not mean to say that this difficulty could not be over-come, but at the moment the most likely thing seems to be again that there was a common tradition. The comment of Barr concerning the age of the tradition of a covenant with Abraham may provide a suggestion for future investigation. Is it possible that there was a covenant form in nomadic times which was the ancestor of both treaty and covenant and which would explain the relationship which exists between them?[190] There will almost certainly also be more discussion yet on the possible differences in *intent* between treaty and covenant.

The last question concerns the age and authorship of the Decalogue. If Gerstenberger's thesis on the origin of apodictic law can be applied to the clauses of the Decalogue, then at least some of what later came to be the Decalogue was older than Moses. But Gerstenberger's work also means, as far as the authorship is concerned, that it is unlikely that Moses had a

[190] On covenants in Genesis, see now Dennis J. McCarthy, 'Three Covenants in Genesis', *CBQ* 26, 1964, pp. 179–189.

direct hand in the Decalogue, at least in the form of anything like a one-man authorship, either for the individual clauses or for the series as a whole. Perhaps his opinion that the Decalogue in complete series may not have existed until the time of the Exile is somewhat too extreme, though he does have a strong argument when he maintains that the direct mention of the 'ten words' is primary only in Deuteronomy. Nor, as far as I see the position correctly, are there any other passages which indisputably show a knowledge of the complete Decalogue; all passages which quote the 'Decalogue' quote only parts of it. If, remembering Alt's remark already quoted[191] on the origin of law in life, it seems more likely that the 'human relationship' clauses[192] would evolve originally in connection with some situation of life directly connected with them rather than that they would have a direct and primary connection with the cult or be composed over a fairly short period of time by one man, this argument also applies to the Decalogue as a full, comprehensive series. That such a comprehensive series should exist also requires some particular circumstance of life, and it seems to me that this is most likely provided by the coming into existence of the amphictyony which, as a new fellowship, had new needs which were the prerequisite for the creation of a full, comprehensive series. It could be said against Gerstenberger that neither the fact that the Decalogue is not indisputably referred to until late, nor that it is not quoted from in full in the whole of the Old Testament, necessarily means that it did not exist before that. The strength of his position is, however, that it would probably have been a gradual process which was not necessarily completed shortly after the Conquest, and which may possibly have taken a considerable time to reach completion. In any case, the time after the Conquest would seem to be the prerequisite for the commencement of the creation of the Decalogue in its whole comprehensiveness, though it can certainly be said that the origins of the individual clauses and of the shorter series probably go back to Mosaic times and even before that.

Some of the views surveyed above and the conclusions which have been drawn from them are considerably different from those

---

[191] 'Ursprünge', *KS* I, p. 284; see above, p. 54.
[192] Matters could of course be different for commandments which have a more direct connection with the cult.

which, up till now, have usually been held about the Decalogue. For this reason, it seems to me to be necessary to make some attempt, here and now, to present some theological considerations, and, since the new approach to the Decalogue raises matters fundamental to the whole question of law in the Old Testament, it is not possible to confine such considerations to the Decalogue alone. Indeed, some of the matters that have been raised above seem to me to contain important consequences for our faith today.[193] It will probably be thought by some that some of the views mentioned above are too 'this-worldly' in contrast to those which are usually held about the Decalogue. Certainly, there is a good deal, particularly in Gerstenberger's work, which seems at first to run counter to widely-held views concerning the importance of seeing law within the context of God's grace. For instance, though he agrees with Joachim Begrich[194] that covenant and prohibitions are two different things, he criticizes the 'Protestant' tone with which Begrich proclaims 'freedom from the law' and 'the character of grace' of the original, genuine covenant idea. For, Gerstenberger says,[195] the making of the covenant in the Old Testament always presupposes that both partners bind themselves to an obligation. That is, the prescriptions have to be kept here too. This passage taken alone might give the impression that Gerstenberger thinks of Old Testament law as something absolute, something which is demanded and which just has to be kept. But, as becomes clear from the conclusions at the end of the work,[196] this is not his intention. Rather he wants to make clear that there can be no possibility of subtracting God's grace from the commandments themselves—it is with the demands of the commandments that God's grace becomes known. That is, as he expresses it, it is not possible to equate the covenant with grace, and then the commandments with law. The discrepancy between covenant and commandment, in the way in which it has been understood in Protestantism, does not exist in the Old Testament. The covenant comes to expression in the commandments; in the context of the covenant, the commandments are the expression of the faithful relationship between persons. It is not possible to

[193] See also now, W. Eichrodt, 'Bund und Gesetz', *Gottes Wort und Gottes Land*, pp. 30–49.

[194] 'Berit', *ZAW* 60, 1944, p. 7 = Begrich, *Gesammelte Studien zum Alten Testament*, Munich, 1964, p. 62.

[195] *Apodiktisches Recht*, pp. 105 f.   [196] *Ibid.*, pp. 145 ff.

subtract the commandments from the covenant and to be left with pure divine grace. The commandment came only gradually into connection with the covenantal formula, but this does not mean that the relationship of fellowship is turned round into a legal understanding, for it is just because the 'demand' is an integral element of every act of covenant-making, that this growing together is possible. The good law, the only intention of which is to preserve the covenantal relationship, develops into its opposite only when it seeks to become the means of forcing the fellowship which as a matter of fact cannot be forced since it can only come about through the free choice of the partners. As far as the connection between law within the covenant and law outside it is concerned, e.g. in the Wisdom literature, it is usual to speak of the rules of Wisdom as being empirical, rational and human, as distinct from the supernatural law conditioned by revelation. But this distinction is a modern one, and this investigation has demonstrated that the dialectic between revelation and reason is foreign to the Old Testament. In substance, the exhortatory word of Wisdom and the legal prohibitions are identical. Certainly, the divine revelation on Sinai plays the decisive role in the faith of Israel, but this and other revelations of the patriarchal narratives are only the magnetic pole around which the old traditions come together in a new order. The ethos of the clan does not even need to be reformed drastically when it comes into the sphere of the Yahweh religion. It is, however, necessary that these good prohibitions (of stealing, murdering etc.) be placed in a relationship to Yahweh so that they come under his aegis. Israel has no impersonal law which, of itself, brings the victory. What is good is involved with persons; Yahweh and men are its authors and guardians.

It seems clear to me that the consequence of this is *not* that the Old Testament law is absolute, that it just has to be kept. But it is also clear that the consequence is that God's grace cannot be abstracted from the demand made on us. It is within this very demand connected with people as they are that the grace of God is most likely to become manifest. Certainly, the danger is always present (and probably it is the greatest danger) that the fulfilling of the demand will be turned into a proud, self-satisfied legalism. Thus, it has to be said that the relationship of grace is not created by the keeping of the demand. But it also has to be said that it is

seeing the necessity for the demand which leads to the grace of
God which itself provides the relationship where the demand can
be met. It is indeed here above all, in connection with the demand
made, that God's grace is known and accepted as the prerequisite
which comes before man's effort, and where it is not merely an
object of belief. This means that there is a second danger which is
present even in such a statement as 'God's grace precedes law'.
The danger is that the grace of God is so abstracted that a faith of
knowledge results which has nothing to do with present needs.
This danger, so expressed, can apply even to those who might
think of Gerstenberger's remarks above as applying only to a
particular theological tradition (i.e. Lutheran), and who have no
thought of making a radical distinction between law and grace.
For, in practice, this distinction is also made when we make
God's grace prevenient in such a way that we have to see it before
we come to God's demand on us. The very stressing of the
prevenience of God's grace can in this way itself become a new
law. It is a law when we are merely making sure that we are
following a theological fashion without, however, seeing for
ourselves what it means for the things which are happening now
in our lives together. Perhaps Israel sometimes ran into this
danger when she saw God's grace almost entirely in mighty acts of
history, so that some such approach as that of the Wisdom literature was really a necessary corrective. As far as the present is
concerned, the fact that a person, when challenged by another
person who is also involved about some matter, often reacts with
such words as 'that is a matter between God and me alone', or
'only God can do that for me', shows that we can use some idea of
the grace of God to do nothing less than avoid him! Neither grace
nor the demand made on us can be regarded as more important or
more primary than the other. In fact, this very statement is misleading in as far as it gives the impression that they are necessarily
two different things. They always belong together. God's grace
can only be given to us in the demand made on us, and in receiving
the gift, we are freed from the slavery of that performance in our
own strength which can only lead to proud and self-satisfied
legalism.

What has been said so far on the conclusions which Gerstenberger draws, concerns the stage when the law was fitted into the
context of the covenant, and as stated, it is clear that it is not his

intention to say that the law is absolute, but that grace and law belong together. But at least something of this dimension is not lacking either for the time when the prohibitions and the commandments, in the ethos of the clan, were not part of the Yahweh faith. Gerstenberger states[197] that if the phrasing of almost all the prohibitions as the speech of Yahweh is secondary, then it is unlikely that they originated in the Covenant Festival and that they were always supported by Yahweh's absolute authority. It is a patriarchal institution which is the authority behind them. But he also states[198] that though the prohibitions were the authoritative commands of the elders of the clan, they do not receive their authority so much from their power as individuals as from the sanctified order which they represent.

Gerstenberger also says[199] that in this patriarchal period the prohibitions and commands do not even have the intention of forcing observance but of laying it close to the heart. He could, of course, have said this just as well for the time of the covenant, and it is not a contradiction of his own view that the prescriptions have to be kept. The observance intended cannot be forced, though, because of the relationship aimed at between *this* God and man, the grace just has not been accepted unless it results in their being kept. It is in the light of the gospel of Jesus Christ that this can be completely understood, because, from this, we can add something else: this grace has not been accepted unless there is the awareness, expressed in confession and repentance, that they have *not* been kept, and it is this above all which will make the keeping of them possible. It is, indeed, in this sense that it can be said that faith has nothing to do with morals at all! Morals as actions which we perform in our own strength, and of which we therefore cannot help being proud, have nothing to do with faith; though the faith which results from the acceptance of God's grace is itself expressed, and itself accepted again and again, in whole relationships with other people.

Thus, even for this early period, Gerstenberger's work does not make it inevitable that the prohibitions and commands have to be seen as something existing in themselves, though it does mean that the formulation of the demand came about in a much more

---

[197] *Apodiktisches Recht*, pp. 60 f; see above, p. 47.
[198] *Ibid.*, p. 110; see above, p. 50.
[199] *Ibid.*, p. 26; see above, pp. 45 f.

'secular' way than is often supposed. It means too, and for this very reason, that an attempt such as Eichrodt's[200] to base the original connection between Yahweh's revelation and the prohibitions on systematic theological considerations is misguided.[201]

From his consideration of the origin of apodictic law, Gerstenberger can also say[202] that it was only subsequently that the historical narrative of the Sinai revelation was added to the lists of commandments[203]—a feature which seems to have no parallel in the ancient Near East. It is no doubt in the light of this statement that Gerstenberger would wish to see the remarks of his very last paragraph concerning the sense in which Israel's law is genuinely and historically unique.[204] He sees his work as demonstrating that it cannot be maintained, as it often is, that that law is either better or more moral than that of Israel's neighbours, or that it is unique because it is revealed. This is not to deny the historical uniqueness of every culture, but historical peculiarities come out of common ground, and the ethos of the clan comes out of such a common ground. In one way it is, perhaps, a pity that Gerstenberger ends on this note, because it rather takes away from the importance, which he himself has discussed, of what Israel's law became in the context of the covenant, and he has also said that the addition of the Sinai revelation is without parallel in the ancient Near East. However, this does not mean that Israel's law is either more moral or better, but something quite different. Israel's law which was brought into the context of the covenant comes to express fully that which was already inherent in it: the necessity of the framework of relationship which breaks through that which is merely

[200] W. Eichrodt, *Theology of the Old Testament* I, ETr., London, 1961.

[201] Gerstenberger, *op. cit.*, p. 110.

[202] *Ibid.*, p. 143; see above, p. 54.

[203] A further implication of Gerstenberger's work which can be mentioned only by the way is that, if the Decalogue commandments are earlier than Sinai, then it cannot be argued from them, and in connection with the mention of the Exodus in Ex. 20.2, that the Exodus and Sinai traditions always belonged together. All commandments standing in the vicinity of the Sinai narrative did not necessarily belong originally to the Sinai tradition. Even if they did, Gerstenberger's attempt to show that the original connection between the prologue and *all* the commandments is by no means certain, would still have to be reckoned with.

Gerstenberger's statement that it was only later that the historical narrative of the Sinai revelation was added to the commandments, could perhaps be put more correctly in this way: the addition of the Exodus tradition was later, and it was only after that that the Sinai narrative was added.

[204] *Op. cit.*, p. 204.

moral. In any case, Gerstenberger is concerned here with the stage before the covenant, and the point he wishes to make is clear and, in my opinion, correct. It comes to this: that God does not make himself known in an exclusive manner, or in a way which is always something 'special', but in and through the lives of people in their everyday form which may not be so different from those of other peoples. This is the implication of the origin of the Decalogue clauses in the clan ethos, and to see how this happened in this seemingly 'secular' life is actually a gain, because it gives us hope that God may work in and through us now. It is just this hope which we cannot have when we are so preoccupied with 'putting God first' or waiting for something 'special' that we do not give him a chance to make known to us his grace in connection with what we actually are and do. God is active not in a sphere removed from us but in our lives with other people, and in accepting him just here, we learn to know him as the Person who is continually seeking to create the new life between us that we cannot create alone.[205]

[205] On the question of the special character of the Decalogue among the various religions, see also Stamm's concluding remarks below, pp. 112 ff.

II

EXEGESIS

1. 'I am Yahweh, your God'

THE first three words of the prologue to the Decalogue, *'ānōkī yhwh 'elōhekā*, make three translations possible:

1. 'I am Yahweh, your God.'
2. 'I, Yahweh, am your God.'
3. 'Besides me, Yahweh, your God, who brought you out of the land of Egypt, you shall have no other gods.'

In the last case, the words *'ānōkī yhwh* (I am Yahweh), which stand at the head of the clause, are understood as an emphatic prolepsis of the suffix of 'besides me' (*'al pānāy*). The prologue thus loses its independence, since it is absorbed into the first commandment. Some would maintain[1] that this opinion can be supported by pointing out that the Decalogue would then become a unified composition containing only commandments and prohibitions. Nevertheless, this understanding is too forced and artificial to be convincing. There thus remain those two possibilities which are closely connected with one another: 'I am Yahweh, your God', or 'I, Yahweh, am your God' which have both found their advocates.[2] The text alone does not provide a solution, though the case for the first possibility is strengthened by the preference of the Greek and Latin translations of the Old Testament (Septuagint and Vulgate). And this would indeed seem to be the correct interpretation, as Zimmerli has shown in

[1] Thus Arno Poebel, *Das appositionell bestimmte Pronomen der ersten Person Sing. in den westsemitischen Inschriften und im Alten Testament*, Chicago, 1932, p. 55.

[2] The first version is given by the Septuagint, the Vulgate, Luther and the Zürich Bible [and by AV and RSV. Tr.]. The second is preferred by, among others, Alt, 'Ursprünge', *KS* I, p. 329, n. 2, Noth, *GSAT*, p. 58, Buber, *Moses*, London, 1946, pp. 135 f (Harper Torchbooks ed., New York, 1958, p. 135), and, with special emphasis, Elias Auerbach, *Moses*, Amsterdam, 1953, p. 199.

his article on the formula 'I am Yahweh'.[3] He quotes in this
connection Ps. 50.7, 'I am Yahweh, your God', a passage which
certainly looks back to the beginning of the Decalogue. In
Hebrew, this is *'elōhīm 'elōhekā 'ānōkī*, which, since we are in the
so-called 'Elohistic Psalter',[4] was originally *yhwh 'elōhekā 'ānōkī*,
which can only be translated by 'I am Yahweh, your God'.
Thus 'I' is subject, and the name of God is predicate. If that
is the case in Ps. 50.7, then it cannot be otherwise in the
introduction to the Decalogue. 'I am Yahweh, your God'
will thus be the rendering which corresponds to the original
meaning.

In the article just mentioned, Zimmerli has traced the origin of
the formula 'I am Yahweh', and he comes to the conclusion that it
was at home in the Priestly literature and that it was taken up by
Ezekiel and especially by Deutero-Isaiah. In the latter, it is the
most lofty declaration which Yahweh can make about himself—a
polemical demonstration against the gods, and a merciful con-
solation to Israel. In the Priestly literature, apart from the call of
Moses in Ex. 6, the formula occurs especially linked with prescriptions in the Holiness Code (Lev. 17–26), which leads one to
presume that it had its place in the cult in the proclamation of law
spoken by the priest. This is confirmed by Ps. 50.7, where the 'I
am Yahweh, your God' stands at the beginning of an address by
God in the course of which allusion is made to the seventh and
eighth commandments. Thus the formula 'I am Yahweh' also
leads us to conclude that the Decalogue had its place in a festival or
cultic celebration. As we have seen, the review of salvation history,
with the deliverance from Egypt at the central position, belonged
to this, as did the exhortatory paranesis. Accordingly, the proclamation of law in the Decalogue was seen in the light of the
deliverance from Egypt as a result of the sequence of the festive
liturgy, and the historical emphasis was given early, perhaps before
the clause 'who brought you out of Egypt' belonged to the con-
stituents of the Decalogue. The Lord's giving of commands is
authorized by the act of deliverance; he has behind him a historical
demonstration which, as Deutero-Isaiah above all brings out, the

---

[3] 'Ich bin Jahwe', *GAT*, pp. 204 f = *GO*, pp. 36 f.
[4] That is Pss. 42–83, in the text of which an original 'Yahweh' was replaced, in the great majority of cases, though not without exception, by the
term, *'elōhīm*, the Hebrew word for 'God'.

other gods do not have. The contrast between salvation history and timeless myth here comes into view.

ADDITIONS

Lohfink has a section on what he calls 'Decalogue language' (*Dekalogsprache*).[5] From the prologue, it seems to him that the expression 'house of bondage' (*bēt ʿᵃbādim*) in particular is exclusively Decalogue language. The passages outside the Decalogue and Deut. 5–8 where this occurs all appear to him to be influenced by Decalogue language in one way or another. This state of affairs would mean either that there was a language formed on the model of the Decalogue, or that there was a language of a circle of traditionalists which originates from both the Decalogue and Deut. 5–8 and which is most clearly formulated in the Decalogue.

David Daube[6] sees an application to the whole Exodus story of the social laws and customs familiar to the authors from their daily world, and one of the motifs associated with this application is that of a change of master which, in his opinion, is introduced in the opening of the Ten Commandments.

Attention has already been drawn to the point which Gerstenberger makes that only the first two commandments are expressed with the 'I' of Yahweh.[7] This makes it likely that, originally, the prologue was bound up with these only, but it does not mean that the whole of the Decalogue could not have been brought into intimate union with the prologue later. In addition to this, however, it has to be said that the whole trend of his work, and the kind of remarks which he makes, for instance, about the impossibility of subtracting the commandments and being left with pure grace,[8] throw doubt on such formulations as that of W. J. Harrelson[9] concerning the prologue being an essential part of the commandments: 'The saving action of Yahweh is the prior reality; grace is prior to law.' The present writer's remarks on the necessity of seeing the grace of God alongside of and simultaneously with what concerns people are also relevant here.[10]

[5] *Das Hauptgebot*, pp. 100 f.
[6] D. Daube, *The Exodus Pattern in the Bible*, London, 1963, pp. 42 f.
[7] *Apodiktisches Recht*, pp. 57 ff; see above, p. 46.
[8] *Ibid.*, pp. 145 f; see above, pp. 70 f.
[9] Article 'Ten Commandments', *IDB* IV, p. 569b.   [10] See above, pp. 71 f.

2. *'You shall have no other gods beside me'*

In the wording of this commandment, the version 'You shall
have no other gods beside me' is familiar to us.[11] 'Beside me'
is the translation of Hebrew *'al pānāy*. This does, in fact, repeatedly
mean 'near by', 'at the side of a place', so that from that standpoint
the usual translation can be justified. Now and then, however,
these Hebrew words carry a hostile undertone, as in Gen. 16.12
in the promise to Ishmael: 'and he shall dwell over against all his
kinsmen' (*'al pᵉnē kol-'eḥāw*) which is repeated in a similar way in
Gen. 25.18. This hostile tone comes out even more clearly in the
prescription of family law in Deut. 21.16, in which, in the case of
marriage with two wives, the second-born son, whose mother is
the loved wife, may not be assigned the right of the first-born in
preference to (*'al pᵉnē*) the real first-born, the son of the disliked
wife. From the basis of this passage, it is possible to consider
with Albright[12] whether the first commandment is not to be
translated by 'Thou shalt not prefer other gods to me.' There are
also other passages (Nahum 2.2; Ps. 21.13) in which *'al pᵉnē* means
'against' (in the hostile sense), and that leads to the rendering of the
'al pānāy in the commandment by 'in defiance of me' (*mir zum
Trotz*). This was first suggested by Eduard König, and was taken
up by Ludwig Koehler.[13]

This 'in defiance of me', which has since been popular, is a
probable interpretation but not the only one which is possible.

As far as the content of the commandment is concerned, there
are exegetes who believe that they owe it to Moses to see this as a
confession which is already monotheistic.[14] This, however, is not

[11] [I.e. in the German-speaking world (*neben mir*). The usual translation in
English is 'before me' which lies, as it were, a stage before the translation of
Albright, 'Thou shalt not prefer other gods to me' referred to below. RSV
offers the alternative 'besides me' in the sense, I presume, of 'in addition to
me'. On these and other possibilities, see Albright's remarks in the passage
referred to in the following note. Tr.]

[12] W. F. Albright, *From the Stone Age to Christianity*, 2nd ed., Baltimore,
1946, p. 331, n. 29 (Doubleday Anchor Books, New York, 1957, p. 297, n. 29).

[13] König, *Das Deuteronomium*, Leipzig, 1917, pp. 86 f; Koehler, 'Der
Dekalog', *ThR*, NS 1, 1929, p. 174; also in *Lexicon in Veteris Testamenti
Libros*, Leiden, 1953, p. 767b.

[14] Recently in particular Albright, *op. cit.*, pp. 196 ff (Doubleday Anchor
Books, pp. 257 ff). Also O. Procksch, *Theologie des Alten Testaments*, Gütersloh,
1950, pp. 82, 92 and 605. On the last-mentioned page, he defines monotheism

correct. It has against it the wording of the commandment which
does not deny the existence of other gods, but only refuses to
recognize their legitimacy for Israel. Moreover, this opinion is
dependent on a false estimate of monotheism, as though this had
already become a central confession of faith in the Old Testament,
as it did later in Judaism and Islam. It is known that this is not
so, since it was not until late—in Deutero-Isaiah—that the Old
Testament came to purely monotheistic statements denying the
existence of the gods alongside the true God. Consequently,
the decision between Yahweh and the gods does not fall into the
sphere of the intellect, as though it were simply a matter of
choosing between reason and unreasonableness, but it is rather
one of trust and obedience which, going beyond knowledge,
claims above all man's volition. The situation presupposed in the
first commandment, and in a great deal of the rest of the Old
Testament as well, can be described by the term known in the
comparative study of religions as monolatry. By this is meant a
polytheistic way of thinking according to which there are not
several gods in a particular circle of worshippers or a particular
nation, but only one—a divinity who tolerates or presupposes
another divinity in another circle of worshippers or another
nation. To speak of monolatry in connection with the first commandment is certainly more adequate than to seek to retain the
concept of monotheism. Certainly, even this does not do complete
justice to the facts of the case in the Old Testament, since the
dynamism of Israelite faith does not receive its sufficient due
within the tolerant static thinking of monolatry. This dynamism
finds its expression in the first commandment being brought
repeatedly into connection with the reference to Yahweh's zeal (or
jealousy). As we shall see when expounding the second commandment, this is present in the Decalogue itself, since the clause
concerning Yahweh's jealousy reaches back beyond the second
commandment to the first. We also have it in the ancient prescription of Ex. 34.14: 'you shall worship no other god, for Yahweh,
whose name is Jealous, is a jealous God.' A similar statement can

as the most important early fact (*Urdatum*) of Old Testament faith in God—
not, however, without a certain qualification. On the whole problem,
reference can now be made to the thorough treatment by Rowley, 'Moses and
Monotheism', *From Moses to Qumran*, London, 1963, pp. 35–63. [This was
first published in German in *ZAW* 69, 1957, pp. 1–21, where material
previously published in *ExpT* 41, 1949–50, pp. 333–338 was utilized. Tr.]

also be found in Deut. 6.14 f. As the jealous God, Yahweh is the exclusive God who does not tolerate any opposing power alongside him—first, no opposing power in the circle of people which has been chosen and separated by him, and then no such power in the whole world. From the very beginning, the faith of Israel was directed to this conclusion, which was implicit as early as the J creation story (Gen. 2) and became explicit in the polemic against the idols in Deutero-Isaiah (Isa. 40–55). Even with regard to the first commandment, then, we must speak of a dynamic monolatry which had the seeds of monotheism within it.

A novel understanding of the first commandment is offered by Reventlow.[15] According to him, the commandment is not to be translated, as is usual, as an exhortation, but as an assertion: 'you have no other gods beside me.' The point is the victory of Yahweh over the foreign gods, which can only be proclaimed and not demanded of man. It remains to be seen whether this explanation will find wide support. In our opinion, its philological basis is not sufficient, and the fact that the ancient translations render the first commandment with the same future form as the other commandments also tells against it.

ADDITIONS

A comment by von Rad[16] is worthy of note. Referring to the commandment in Deuteronomy, he says that it is '*the* commandment *par excellence* for Israel'; its stringency has no parallel in the whole history of religion, and more or less all the expressions of the faith of Yahweh were determined by it.[17]

3. 'You shall not make yourself a graven image'

In recent times the background of this commandment in comparative religion has been increasingly clarified since it has been more clearly recognized what the essence of a divine image is.[18]

---

[15] *Gebot und Predigt*, pp. 25 ff.

[16] *Deuteronomy*, p. 56.

[17] On this commandment, see also now, R. Knierim, 'Das erste Gebot', *ZAW* 77, 1965, pp. 20–39.

[18] A particularly valuable contribution to this has been made by Karl-Heinz Bernhardt, *Gott und Bild*, Berlin, 1956, pp. 24 ff.

There are indeed unambiguous statements about this in the Old Testament itself. They begin indirectly in the story of the ark (I Sam. 5) with the ridiculing of the image of Dagon which has fallen broken to the ground before the ark.

These statements continue in open derision in Hosea (8.4) in the sentence: 'With their silver and gold they made idols for their own destruction', and they come to their climax in Jer. 10, and in Deutero-Isaiah (Isa. 44) in the ironic description of the making of idols by workmen. The last-mentioned texts have the effect of making the worship of idols into self-glorifying stupidity. This is on the whole a late rationalizing view of things which contains a profound truth even if it does not do justice to the spiritual content which the worship of divine images once had. The image was actually above all the dwelling place of the divine reality. It was not the material any more than the form which was the decisive thing, but precisely this divine reality which animates the image in taking up residence there. This high and spiritual understanding could easily be demonstrated from Egyptian and Sumerian–Babylonian texts.[19] We cannot do this at this moment, but it is sufficient that we have at least made reference to the original meaning of the divine image. This alone makes it possible to imagine what its prohibition meant in the way of religious renunciation.

The prescription in the Decalogue which originally only contained the words: 'You shall not make yourself a graven image' (*pesel*), has its parallels in the Old Testament in Ex. 20.23, 'You shall not place anything alongside me; you shall not make for yourself gods of silver and gods of gold', Ex. 34.17, 'You shall make for yourself no molten gods' (*massēkā*), and Deut. 27.15, 'Cursed be the man who makes a graven or molten image' (*pesel ūmassēkā*). The relationship between these versions has been much discussed, above all with reference to the fact that, in the Decalogue, the graven image is prohibited and not, as in the other passages, the molten image as well, or the molten image only. Does that justify the conclusion that the Decalogue has particularly ancient conditions in view, since only divine images carved from wood or hewn from stone were known, but not those cast from metal? Though this seems obvious, even the linguistic evidence does not necessarily make this conclusion compelling

[19] Bernhardt, *Gott und Bild*, pp. 28 ff and 34 ff.

since, though the Hebrew *pesel* does predominate with the meaning 'graven image', it is, however, also used of the molten image (Isa. 40.19; 44.10). In addition to this, there is the nature of the Decalogue itself. As we have seen, in apodictic law it is contrasted, as a so-called comprehensive series, with the special series. A comprehensive, generalizing tendency therefore suits it; accordingly, its wording will from the beginning have prohibited not only a particular kind of image, but the image as such. We have here an extended understanding of the word *pesel* which is unmistakably expressed in the Old Testament itself through the clauses which were added to the originally short commandment.

Which divine being did the prohibited images represent? In an article on images of Yahweh to which much attention has been paid, the Dutch scholar H. Th. Obbink has advocated the view that it was not a matter of images of Yahweh but of Canaanite cultic images which might have been set up in Yahweh sanctuaries.[20] For, as a matter of fact, there were no real representations of Yahweh in Israelite religion. Micah's image (Judg. 17–18) was an idol, and even the calves set up by Jeroboam (I Kings 12) were not symbols of Yahweh but those of the Canaanite storm god, Hadad; the calf was thought of as the pedestal of the god standing invisibly on it. Obbink thinks that it is only if Canaanite gods were in view that the reference to divine jealousy in the second commandment could be meaningful; for 'how can Yahweh be jealous if Israel makes an image of him and bows down before this image of Yahweh? But if Israel shows the honour due to Yahweh to other gods, then Yahweh's jealousy is stirred up, since he cannot tolerate that his honour should be given to other gods.'[21] With these presuppositions, the second commandment gains the following meaning: 'You shall keep the worship of Yahweh pure and not disfigure it with all kinds of heathen material.'[22] This is a forceful interpretation which deserves a thorough investigation. If this is done, however, the thesis must finally be rejected, for two reasons in particular. First, the existence of images of Yahweh in

---

[20] 'Jahwebilder', *ZAW* 47, 1929, pp. 264–274. Reventlow, *op. cit.*, pp. 29 ff, is also of the opinion that the second commandment had originally to do only with images of heathen deities. Images of Yahweh were at first allowed, and only after a time forbidden. It was in connection with this that the application of the second commandment was then extended to representations of Yahweh.

[21] *Op. cit.*, p. 265.   [22] *Ibid.*, p. 274.

Israelite popular religion cannot be contested. The main proof of this is the image of Micah, which, according to the context of the passage, cannot be understood as an idol image, even though it may have appeared as such to a later age. Secondly, the second commandment could be seen exclusively in an anti-Canaanite context if the Decalogue could be derived only from the situation of Israel in Canaan. This, however, is not the case. Its roots are pre-Canaanite, and it has to be taken into consideration that as early as the desert sojourn the prohibition of images was already part of the faith of Yahweh.

If this is correct, then the images prohibited in the Decalogue must have been those of Yahweh, which leads on to the assumption that the worship of Yahweh in its ancient and genuine form was imageless. This is confirmed by the sources since, in the period of desert wandering, they know only the ark as an imageless symbol of guidance. And even after the Conquest, when the ark had become the central focus of the tribes which had been combined in the manner of a league, an amphictyony, their cult continued to be imageless, as the texts relating to Shiloh at the time of the young Samuel (I Sam. 3) and those relating to Jerusalem at the time of David and Solomon (I Sam. 6; I Kings 8) show. The question could now be put thus: did an imageless cult have any need of a prohibition of images? The answer is that the numinous character of the divine image already mentioned means that this was not superfluous. If anyone set up an image of Yahweh, he was founding a new cult, since he placed alongside the ark, as the only legitimate sign of divine presence, another arbitrarily created one. The temptation to do this was never far removed, and the Israelites frequently succumbed to it, since they wished to assure themselves of the divine presence more directly and concretely than the ark allowed. This could take place by erecting a veritable image of Yahweh; the pericope on the golden calf (Ex. 32) is an example. When this happened, syncretistic forms through which Yahweh was represented under cover of Canaanite divinities and their symbols became popular. In the Decalogue, the extension of the second commandment is aiming to counteract this when it adds to the original form entities from the wide realm of the cosmos. This encroaches deeply on man's artistic activity; limitations are set to it at the point where art serves the representation of religious and cultic motifs. The dividing lines here were, however, very fluid, as Solomon's temple with its decorations in plant and animal motifs particularly shows. Unfortunately, we are not in a position to define exactly their relationship to the second commandment. Was the ornamentation of the temple considered to be in harmony with this commandment because what it represented was not directly worshipped? Or do the supplementary clauses to the commandment stand in silent opposition to the artistic elaboration of the temple which, like the whole temple for that matter, was a work of Israelite–Canaanite syncretism?

An important question still remaining is that of the significance of the prohibition of images. The most obvious answer, and one which is frequently given, is that this is to be found in the spiritual understanding of God, and the intention is to distinguish between the world of God and the world of the senses. Beer has even ventured to assert that 'Through the prohibition of images, God is declared to be spirit.'[23] The fact which contradicts this from the very outset is that the Old Testament, which speaks of God in an expressly anthropomorphic way, does not have such a spiritual understanding of God as is here presupposed. Further, this interpretation does not pay enough attention to what the Old Testament itself provides for an interpretation of the commandment. This can be found in the context of the commandment and in the clarifying statements of Deut. 4.

In the context, the short commandment and its subsequent extension are further followed by the exhortation: 'You shall not bow down to them or serve them.' Grammatically, the striking thing here is the plural 'to them', since it can no longer refer to the singular expression 'graven image' (*pesel*) of the preceding verse. Zimmerli has provided the solution to this difficulty in an article on the second commandment[24] where he has recognized that the plural 'to them' refers back behind the second commandment to the first,[25] to be exact, to the words 'other gods' in the clause: 'You shall have no other gods beside me.' It is they who are meant when the supplement to the second commandment gives this warning against bowing down to them and serving them. This insight,

[23] G. Beer, *Exodus*, Tübingen, 1939, p. 100.
[24] 'Das zweite Gebot', *FSAB*, pp. 550–563 = *GO*, pp. 234–248.
[25] This was already recognized by A. Knobel, *Die Bücher Exodus und Leviticus*, Leipzig, 1857, p. 204, and by B. D. Eerdmans, *Alttestamentliche Studien* III, 1910, p. 133.

won in the first place from the grammar, is confirmed by the use of the phrase ('bow down and serve', in Hebrew *hištaḥᵃwā* and *'ābad*.²⁶ It means 'to offer religious worship (*gottesdienstlich verehren*), and it is only used in connection with divinities which are foreign to Israel and forbidden to her. The phrase is never used for the worship of Yahweh, nor for that of the images. The wording of the second commandment, then, is no exception to this; the exhortation 'You shall not bow down to them or serve them' will then really have referred not to the images but to the foreign gods. The reference to Yahweh's jealousy which concludes the second commandment confirms this; this, as we have already had to point out, is the reason given elsewhere too for the prohibition of worshipping foreign gods. From all this, the conclusion cannot be avoided that, whoever added the clauses in question to the second commandment, for him this commandment stood completely in the shadow of the first. He treated the prohibition of images and that of foreign gods as one and the same thing, and thus already shares the understanding which later became usual with Roman Catholics and Lutherans. Such fusion of the commandments would not have been possible if they had not been felt to be intrinsically homogeneous. If the worship of foreign gods was an encroachment on Yahweh's sovereign right of rule over Israel which belonged to him exclusively, then it cannot have been otherwise with the worship of images. 'Yahweh's freedom is impugned in the divine image which man makes for himself.'²⁷ Considering the fact of the ark, this sentence can be ventured even for Israel's early period. It was the only legitimate sign of divine presence. An image meant that the Israelite absolved himself from this order and at the same time took steps to put Yahweh in his power as a numen which was near at hand in the cultic object which he had chosen for himself. It is in general an essential part of the worship of images that man takes the divinity into his power.

In Deut. 4, the reason given for the prohibition of images is that Israel on Horeb did not see any form, but only heard a voice. As von Rad emphasizes,²⁸ a fundamental antithesis is thus worked out, since it means that in her relationship to God Israel

---

²⁶ Zimmerli, *FSAB*, pp. 553 f = *GO*, pp. 237 f.
²⁷ *FSAB*, p. 561 = *GO*, p. 246.
²⁸ G. von Rad, *Old Testament Theology* I, Edinburgh, 1962, p. 216.

unlike other peoples, is not directed towards a cultic image, but only towards Yahweh's word.

ADDITIONS

Reventlow[29] has a criticism to make of the views of Zimmerli which have been outlined above. He thinks that Zimmerli is right in his conclusion that the formula 'bow down and serve' is never used for the worship of Yahweh or of the images but he does not think that it serves the purpose which Zimmerli intends. It is correct that it is a question of the prohibition of foreign gods, but that does not necessarily refer to v. 3 since, in his view,[30] this is not a commandment, but the conclusion of the introductory epiphany; and since v. 5a is obviously the continuation of a commandment, this link cannot come into question. The difficulty disappears in the recognition that v. 5 is a new, subsequent addition which refers not only to *pesel* but also to 'likeness' (*temūnā*). This interpretation depends, of course, on the correctness of Reventlow's thesis about the first commandment; furthermore, since the words *pesel* and *temūnā* are used, it is difficult to see how, on Reventlow's thesis of the separation between the first and second commandments, these can be understood as foreign gods rather than images. It also depends on v. 4b being there before v. 5—a matter which he does not really treat in detail.

Kilian,[31] discussing Lev. 19.4, says that, although the original prohibition of images was directed against images of Yahweh, it now appears mostly in connection with foreign gods and images. If Rowley is correct in his view that Ex. 34.14–28 contains an older decalogue than Ex. 20.1–17,[32] then Lev. 19.4 has likewise preserved this old form—there are no interpretative additions— and it is perhaps to be seen as dependent on Ex. 34.17—if only loosely.

On the significance of the prohibition, von Rad,[33] referring to Deuteronomy, says that it must be understood from the point of

[29] *Gebot und Predigt*, p. 31.
[30] See above, p. 81.
[31] *Literarkritische und formgeschichtliche Untersuchung des Heiligkeitsgesetzes*, pp. 37 f.
[32] 'Moses and the Decalogue', *BJRL* 34, 1951–52, pp. 81–118 = *Men of God*, pp. 1–36.
[33] *Deuteronomy*, p. 57.

view of the function of divine images which was 'to manifest the deity'. There is here a different understanding of the world than that of the ancient Near Eastern religions, for, since it is denied that Yahweh can be portrayed by any form such as those of animals, of constellations, or of man, or that he can be identified with the mythical forces or orders of the world, it means that the world could not be seen as the outward shape of the divinity himself. In an article on aspects of the understanding of the world in the Old Testament,[34] the same writer stresses that it is not the intention of the prohibition of images to further a spiritual worship of God, and that it is not directed against that which is material. As pointed out above, it is more a question of the manifestation of the deity in the image. Something happens between the image and the worshipper; in it the deity in some way communicates with the worshipper. It is here that the meeting between them takes place, and, without the gods and their images, man in the world would be lost. A most interesting point is von Rad's estimate of the lofty character of much image worship which, despite all this—perhaps because of it—Israel still has to reject, for Yahweh was closer to Israel in a much more intimate way, namely in the word of address and in action in history. This means that anthropomorphisms were unavoidable in the expression of Israel's understanding of God, but in the prohibition of images, the boundary between God and the world is drawn differently and much more sharply than was the case in the religions with images. Yahweh was not one of the sustaining forces of the world, not even their sum, but their creator. The prohibition of images is an element from which Israel built up her most rudimentary understanding of God and the world.

Thus—this seems to me to be the consequence—the prohibition of images does not mean an understanding of God which is 'spiritual' in the sense that the material is of a lower order with reference to God—quite the opposite. It means that as soon as the meeting with God is identified in any way whatsoever with a representation of what is seen to be one of the sustaining forces of the world, or just something which is 'above us', man as a matter of fact excludes God from his relationship with his fellows in the material world. The image, whether in an ancient or in a

[34] 'Aspekte alttestamentlichen Weltverständnisses', *EvTh* 24, 1964, pp. 57–73, here 59 ff.

modern sense, puts God and what concerns him into a category which is different from, and above, man in this world, and this, since it avoids the problems of man in the world, is tantamount to having God at one's disposal and control. It is, indeed, the characteristic of images that *they* are 'spiritual', and this means that in those spheres which man, with the help of the image, has ensured are not touched by God, he is left, in fact, with the merely material. It is just in this world without images of any kind that man is most likely to meet God, because, without these, he is truly open to God in what he is, where he is; and where this happens, there is the presupposition for the truly spiritual.

4. *'You shall not take the name of Yahweh in vain'*

It is unanimously agreed that this commandment protects the name of Yahweh from that unlawful use which could take place in the oath, the curse,[35] and in sorcery, and, besides this, 'wherever Israel in any way opened its doors to the cult of another deity'.[36] The commandment, not only from the point of view of its position, but also from that of its content, stands in a particularly close relationship with the prohibition of images. For, like the image, the name of the divinity is also an essential means for gaining power over him. Whoever possesses the name also possesses the person of him who is named. It is for this reason that the names of divinities play a prominent part in incantations, and in ancient oriental literature incantation texts have an important place. In the Old Testament, on the other hand, they are completely lacking, since magic and sorcery are out of the question here. Scholars have spoken of the magical *Weltanschauung* of the ancient Near East, and it is widely held that this was first overcome in the Greek philosophy of nature. But this conquest was through knowledge. It took place before this in Israel through the history of salvation: Yahweh, the God of guidance from the time of the

[35] In Hos. 4.2: 'there is swearing, lying, killing, stealing, and committing adultery', it is certain that allusion is made to the sixth, seventh and eighth commandments, and from this it is likely that the word 'swearing' refers to the third commandment. This means that the Old Testament itself brought this commandment into connection with the curse. [Koehler, *Lexicon in Veteris Testamenti Libros*, p. 49a, gives 'hurl curses' as one meaning for the word in question in Hos. 4.2, *'ālā*. Tr.] On Hos. 4.2, see Hans Walter Wolff, *Dodekapropheton* 1, Neukirchen, 1961, pp. 84 f.
[36] Von Rad, *Old Testament Theology* I, p. 184.

desert, is near to his people; near in the ark, as well as in his name revealed through Moses (Ex. 3 and 6). Nevertheless, he remains free in them both, and does not put himself at the disposal of man. The point is precisely that his nearness is not something given through nature and myth, but that it is established in history through choice (election).

5. 'Remember the sabbath day'

Now, as ever, scholars are striving to clarify the origin of the sabbath, without, however, having come any nearer to the goal. Several theses concerning its origin still stand in opposition to each other, and none of them is really able to solve the mystery.

From the time that it has been known that the fifteenth day of the month was called *šapattu* in Babylon, it has seemed to be the obvious place in which to look for the origins of the sabbath. This seemed particularly likely some decades ago, when scholars, under the overwhelming impression of the newly-won insights from Assyriology, reckoned with a direct influence on Israel by Babylon. Since then it has been possible to come to a clearer understanding of the cultural significance of Canaan and Syria, and for this reason, one has become more cautious in the matter. But despite this, Mesopotamia still plays its role in the question concerning the sabbath. Should there really be a connection between the two, then it must go back to a comparatively early time; for, in the Old Babylonian era, a festival cycle can be found which could be considered as the first step towards the Israelite celebration of the sabbath.[37] Following the course of the moon, the first, seventh, fifteenth and twenty-eighth days of the month were at that time brought into particular prominence as days of special sacrifices, and of these it is the fifteenth which is specified as *šapattu*. If this is accepted as the origin of the biblical sabbath, there remains the question when and how the weekly holy day, which was independent of the course of the moon, developed from it. The term *šapattu* can also be found in later times in Babylonian–Assyrian texts, and, what is more, in the secular sense of 'day of full moon', not in that of 'festival of full moon'.[38] In this connection, calendar-like texts of the tenth and

---

[37] On this, see Benno Landsberger, *Der kultischer Kalender der Babylonier und Assyrer*, Leipzig, 1915, p. 99.   [38] *Ibid.*, p. 131.

seventh centuries[39] name certain days of the month when particular
activities are dangerous for some professions. They are a kind of
day of ill-boding or taboo day which again relates to the course
of the moon. In the tenth century there are nine of them, and in
the seventh five, namely the seventh, fourteenth, nineteenth,
twenty-first, and twenty-eighth. If one ventured to take a step
from here to the biblical sabbath, then it would be an even longer
one than that required from Old Babylonian times. For, in
addition to the disparity in reckoning the days, that is, the
connection with or freedom from the phases of the moon, there
is now added that of content, since it is the joyfully celebrated
sabbath which confronts the gloomy Assyrian taboo days. As is
known from Deut. 16, the old Israelite cult was of a joyful
character, and the pre-exilic sabbath will have been of like nature.
It was later that its observance became more strict and stern. It
can at least be considered whether, perhaps during the Exile, the
observance of the Babylonian taboo days might have exercised an
influence in this direction. But we cannot go further than this,[40]
since, as has been noted, the Babylonian taboo days are too
different from the Israelite sabbath.

There is another theory about the origin of the sabbath which is
connected with the view which seeks the beginnings of the faith
of Yahweh among the Kenites, the so-called Kenite hypothesis.
This suggestion was first brought forward by the Dutchman
Eerdmans,[41] and has continued to be advocated by Koehler,[42]
Budde,[43] and Rowley,[44] among others. This hypothesis sees the
Kenites as a tribe of smiths who owed allegiance to Yahweh, and
it brings together Ex. 35.3, which prohibits the making of fire
on the sabbath, and Num. 15.32, which tells of the stoning of a
man who gathered wood on the sabbath, no doubt with the
intention of making fire. The emphasis on work to do with fire

[39] On these, see Stephen Langdon, *Babylonian Menologies and the Semitic
Calendars*, London, 1935, pp. 86 f.
[40] Against Norman H. Snaith, *The Jewish New Year Festival*, London, 1947,
pp. 118 ff.
[41] B. D. Eerdmans, 'Der Sabbath', in *Vom Alten Testament. Karl Marti zum
70. Geburtstage gewidmet*, ed. by K. Budde, Giessen, 1925, pp. 79–83.
[42] L. Koehler, 'Der Dekalog', *ThR*, NS 1, 1929, p. 181.
[43] K. Budde, 'The Sabbath and the Week', *Journal of Theological Studies* 30,
1929, pp. 1–15.
[44] H. H. Rowley, 'Moses and the Decalogue', *BJRL* 34, 1951–52, pp. 114 f
= *Men of God*, pp. 32 ff.

as one which was forbidden on the sabbath is said to belong to the environment of the old Kenite tribe of smiths, and the sabbath would have been a day of rest which was originally Kenite, and which Moses took over, giving new reasons for it and providing it with a broader content. This thesis is so ingenious that one is very willing to consider it again and again, but it is at the same time so uncertain, that it does not necessarily lead to complete conviction.

One must unhesitatingly reject, on the other hand, the view that the sabbath, in Israel as well as in Babylon, was at first a 'day of full moon', and that it was not until the Exile or even in post-exilic times that there developed from it a holy day which was independent of the moon, and which came up at intervals of seven days.[45] For how is this transition to be explained? And if the day of full moon had really been celebrated in Israel for centuries, would there not have remained, even in later times, a memory of the former situation? We may search for this, however, in vain.

The preceding conjectures have one thing in common: they all somehow derive the sabbath from astronomical and cultic data. In distinction from these we find attempts to trace the origin of the sabbath in the economic and social sphere. Among others, Ernst Jenni[46] is a representative of this point of view. He draws attention to the market days 'which can recur at intervals of three, four, five, six, eight or ten days. . . . In general, the market day is a day of rest. As a day of rest on which people come together in crowds, it can develop into a festival day.' Jenni is of the opinion that, as the closest parallel in ethnology and in the comparative study of religions, the market day may well deserve consideration as a hypothesis for the reconstruction of the prehistory of the Israelite sabbath. 'The market day, from the religiously neutral day of rest to that invested with many and various taboos and sub-ordinated to a particular god, plays a role among very different peoples. That there is no evidence for the interval of seven days may be fortuitous and, in any case, does not stand in the way of the hypothesis. . . .' This hypothesis deserves every consideration, even if, as the last sentence shows, it is not the key which has opened the door once and for all.

---

[45] So J. Meinhold, 'Zur Sabbathfrage', *ZAW* 48, 1930, pp. 121–138.

[46] E. Jenni, *Die theologische Begründung des Sabbatgebotes im Alten Testament*, Zollikon, 1956, pp. 12 f.

This series of suggestions which has been made concerning the origin of the sabbath could be continued still further.[47] We leave this subject in order to pass on to the sabbath as an Israelite institution. Fortunately, insight into its nature is not dependent on knowledge concerning its origins. From ancient times the sabbath occurs in the Old Testament as a weekly day of rest. It has always been a matter for comment that, of all the festivals, it alone is mentioned in the Decalogue, a fact which has been brought forward as the main argument for the Decalogue's origin during the Exile. But the preferential treatment given to the sabbath is not connected with the date of the Decalogue, but with its function in the festival. It was here read out, perhaps by the priests, before the participators in the cult. These were laymen to whom the Decalogue gave direction for their life after their return from the festival. The sabbath, which each could observe, belonged to this life, but the three great yearly festivals (Unleavened Bread, Weeks and Tabernacles) did not. They towered over and beyond the sphere of the individual, and the task of carrying them out was largely entrusted to the priests. We can see too that it was not because the Decalogue was alien to the cult, or even hostile to it, that the usual festivals are absent from its commandments, but rather because the cult forms its naturally presupposed background.

The history of the sabbath in Israel is, as is known, that of an increasingly deepened discernment, which recognized first its social significance and then its significance within the history of salvation, which relates to the whole cosmos. This is set forth in detail in the excellent work of Jenni already mentioned.

ADDITIONS

J. Morgenstern[48] sees the origin of the sabbath in an agricultural calendar which was based on the successive stages of the agricultural process. Its basic unit of time-reckoning was the week of seven days. This was one of the Canaanite institutions which the Israelites borrowed, but it was also current among the Eastern

---

[47] On this see J. Botterweck, 'Der Sabbat im Alten Testamente', *Theologische Quartalschrift* 134, 1954, pp. 134–136 and 448–457, and H.-J. Kraus, *Worship in Israel*, pp. 81 ff.

[48] Article 'Sabbath', *IDB* IV, pp. 135a–141a.

Semites, and the Babylonian *šabattū/šapattū* (as it is transliterated here) was derived from it too. Thus, far from the origin of the sabbath being in the *šabattū*, they were both derived from a common source. Morgenstern deals with the difficulty of this being originally an evil day by saying that the Israelites gradually transformed it into a day of gladness, and later, by saying that the commandment in its original negative form has the essential connotation of abstention. Both these are possible, though a negative form does not necessarily imply an essential connotation of abstention. But if, because of this difficulty, the thesis does not sound quite so convincing as Jenni's, caution has to be exercised because of our lack of knowledge.

In his consideration of this commandment, Reventlow[49] maintains that it does not belong to the apodictic series; its formulation in Ex. 20.8, which varies from that of the other commandments, is derived from the Torah. G. Fohrer, in his summary of the book,[50] says, however, that the missing apodictic prohibition is to be found in v. 10b.

Mowinckel,[51] speaking of Ex. 34.21 which he considers to be old, finds its most likely explanation in its being concerned with leaving off work at the time of ploughing and harvest. These were critical times when one had to guard against the influence of 'dangerous' days. The sabbath here seems to have had a particular connection with work in the field, and Mowinckel thinks that an old taboo has gradually become a religious commandment, though the omission of other activities on the sabbath had no such significance.

Kline,[52] arguing for the parallelism of external appearance between the covenant and the vassal treaty, is tempted to see in what he calls 'the sabbath sign' in the midst of the ten words, the equivalent of the suzerain's dynastic seal found on the obverse of the treaty documents. There will be no representation of Yahweh on his seal, but the sabbath is declared to be his 'sign of the covenant' (i.e. in Ex. 31.13–17. These words do not occur in this exact combination, which makes Kline's inverted commas misleading). 'The creator has stamped on world history the sign of the

[49] *Gebot und Predigt*, pp. 55 f.
[50] *ZAW* 74, 1962, p. 361.
[51] *Erwägungen zur Pentateuch Quellenfrage*, Oslo, 1964, p. 93.
[52] *Treaty of the Great King*, pp. 18 f.

sabbath as his seal of ownership and authority.' This is not intimately enough connected with the Decalogue itself to be very convincing.[53]

Von Rad[54] speaks of the sabbath as the day which in its very nature is the one which belongs to God. We do not hear anything about any cultic celebration on this day, and this would point to the fact that its meaning, at least in ancient times, consisted in a demonstrative abstinence from any use of it and in a confessional giving back of the day to Yahweh.

6. '*Honour your father and your mother*'

In the first part of our survey[55] we had occasion to refer to Hans Schmidt's article, 'Mose und der Dekalog', which appeared in 1923 in the Gunkel *Festschrift*. As we come to the fifth commandment, we do so again, for Schmidt is of the opinion[56] that the commandment about honouring parents like the one about the sabbath, must be excluded from the original form of the Decalogue which he reconstructed. One reason for this is that the commandment in question is meant for young people and not, like the other commandments, for the Israelite paterfamilias. Schmidt would have been right if it had been only a matter of considering the small family of modern times in which generally only parents and children live together, but the conditions in ancient Israel were different. The normal unit here was the clan which dwelt together on the inherited land and property. The aged parents lived here together with their adult children, that is with the sons and their dependents; this is the land (*'adāmā*) of which the supplementary clause of promise to the original commandment speaks. From the point of view of this situation, it will be necessary, with Georg Beer,[57] to clarify the precise meaning of the verb 'honour'. Beer writes: 'The aged parents, those over sixty years, whose capacity for work and whose valuation has diminished (Lev. 27.7), are not to be treated harshly by the Israelite; he is not to begrudge them the bread of charity, or force them to leave the house or take the way of voluntary death, or

---

[53] For a thesis which seeks to show the great importance of the sabbath for the deuteronomic version of the Decalogue, see also now N. Lohfink, 'Zur Dekalogfassung von Dt 5', *BZ*, NS 9, 1965, pp. 17–32.

[54] *Deuteronomy*, p. 58.   [55] See above, p. 24.

[56] *EHG*, pp. 81 f and 105.   [57] *Exodus*, p. 102.

even to kill them himself.' These words might appear somewhat blunt, but that they are not going too far is shown by the following maxims from the Book of Proverbs (19.26; 20.20):

> He who does violence to his father and chases away his mother
>   is a son who causes shame and brings reproach.
> If one curses his father or his mother,
>   his lamp will be put out in utter darkness.

The second clause quoted here reminds us that the conjectured original form of the fifth commandment was 'You shall not curse your father or your mother.' It was later transposed into the positive form, and it is this which gives the command its breadth. In this case too Israel learnt to go on to a deeper meaning, as shown, for example, by the paraphrase in the third chapter of Ecclesiasticus.

ADDITIONS

Gerstenberger[58] thinks that the priority of the negative form cannot be proved either for the commandment concerning the sabbath or for that concerning parents. It is possible that both were transmitted from the beginning in a negative and a positive form. This is a stimulus to further thought, but the lack of detail in his treatment means that it is no more.

From the point of view of Deut. 21.18–21, Reventlow[59] thinks that this commandment's sphere of application is more general than that of the respect of the paterfamilias for his aged parents even if he is adult. There is perhaps no reason why both could not have been meant, though this latter understanding might be correct only in as far as special circumstances such as those described in Deut. 21 were involved.

Boecker[60] makes the interesting point that, although the woman's position in law was in many ways very limited, as mother she was equal to the man as father and had full claim on the obedience of the children (Ex. 20.12; Deut. 5.16). This is also shown by Deut. 21.18–21, where the spokesman is certainly the father, but the mother is also mentioned in the formulation 'our son', 'our voice' as a partner who is likewise involved in the matter.

[58] *Apodiktisches Recht*, p. 46.
[59] *Gebot und Predigt*, pp. 65 f.
[60] *Redeformen des Rechtlebens im Alten Testament*, p. 75 and n. 5.

Harrelson[61] thinks of the commandment as a 'bridge' between the two parts of the Ten Commandments, for although it really belongs to the following ones and concerns relations between men, the son's obligation to his parents is a deeply religious one, and comes to be used to describe the relation between Israel and God. He later points out that since the commandment is not merely intended for young children, admonitions to parents to deal properly with their children are proper implications from it (Eph. 6.4; Col. 3.21).

Von Rad[62] points out that, in contrast to the commandment concerning the sabbath, this one gives a promise and not a reason for keeping it. But, according to Old Testament tradition, this promise of life stands over all the commandments (Deut. 4.1; 8.1; 16.20; 30.15 ff), so that later interpreters took a liberty in giving special emphasis to the promise of life here, perhaps in connection with the family's own property.

Johann Gamberoni[63] also makes these points and explains the occurrence of the promise here by saying that it could easily follow the mention of the leading out of Egypt, which occurs in the Deuteronomic version of the commandment on the sabbath, and also that it might have been inserted because the commandment concerning parents could well be in danger of being neglected (Prov. 28.24). He maintains further that every prescription could be motivated from the whole of the covenant. He does not, like Heinz Kremers,[64] think that the formula originated in a cultic association with this commandment, but that it came to it having already a 'spiritualized' meaning. This is a different emphasis, therefore, from von Rad's last-mentioned point. The reasons Gamberoni gives seem to me to range somewhat too loosely from the context of the commandment in Ex. 20 and Deut. 5, and it seems more likely that the promise of life would here be embedded in the particular situation which belongs together with life with parents, that is, the inherited property of the family. Gamberoni also discusses the material on the child–parent relationship in the Old Testament as a whole, and, like

---

[61] Article 'Ten Commandments', *IDB* IV, pp. 569b f and 571a f.

[62] *Deuteronomy*, p. 58.

[63] J. Gamberoni, 'Das Elterngebot im Alten Testament', *BZ*, NS 8, 1964, pp. 161–190.

[64] H. Kremers, 'Die Stellung des Elterngebotes im Dekalog', *EvTh* 21, 1961, pp. 145–161.

Gerstenberger, notes that much of this occurs in the Wisdom literature, particularly in Proverbs.

7. 'You shall not kill'

The sixth commandment, in Hebrew *lō' tirṣaḥ*, is familiar to us in the translation 'You shall not kill'; but 'You shall not murder' is often preferred to this. Neither of them is completely beyond doubt. In the first case, the question arises how a prohibition against killing is related to the wars of Israel which were allowed and even commanded, and it is uncertain in the second case whether the verb *rāṣaḥ*, which is used in the Hebrew in the simple form (*Qal*) could also mean 'murder', since for this sense, one would expect the intensive form (*Piel*). These difficulties were naturally not hidden from an expert like Ludwig Koehler, but he did not think that it was possible to solve them. In his account of the state of research in 1929,[65] he writes that it is difficult to say what was actually and originally meant in the sixth commandment. It is most likely that it was forbidding the Israelite to take the law into his own hands. 'Where an injustice is to be atoned for by the death of the evil-doer, it has to take place through the medium of the community.' But Koehler concluded that, because of a lack of anything concrete to go by, the matter had not got beyond the stage of conjecture. It is surprising that the later author of the Hebrew dictionary hardly gave any consideration to the use of language, which does, after all, provide something to go by. The present writer has made up for this in an article on the sixth commandment,[66] the results of which have in the meantime been accepted, in particular by Albrecht Alt.[67] The word *rāṣaḥ*, which is used in the Decalogue to express killing, is actually a somewhat rare verb when one considers its 46 occurrences in comparison with 165 for *hārag* and 201 for *hēmīt* (*Hiphil* of *mūt* 'to die'). Evidently *hārag* and *hēmīt* were the verbs usually employed to

[65] 'Der Dekalog', *ThR*, NS 1, p. 182.

[66] J. J. Stamm, 'Sprachliche Erwägungen zum Gebot "Du sollst nicht töten" ', *Theologische Zeitschrift* 1, 1945, pp. 81–90. Reference should be made to this article for verification in detail.

[67] 'Das Verbot des Diebstahls im Dekalog', *KS* I, p. 333, n. 1; Reventlow, *Gebot und Predigt*, pp. 71 ff has now also taken over my interpretation, and supplemented it with the view that the verb *rāṣaḥ* originally meant any killing which fell into the sphere of blood revenge.

express killing. This is confirmed by an examination of the use of language in individual cases. *hārag* and *hēmīt* are used for killing one's personal enemy, for murdering him, for killing a political enemy in battle, for killing one who was punishable according to the law, and for death as a judgement of God. By contrast, *rāṣaḥ* only occurs when it is a matter of killing or murdering a personal enemy; only once (Num. 35.30) does it designate the killing of one who is guilty before the law, and it is never used for the killing of the enemy in battle or for the destruction by God of someone who has fallen under his judgement. It can be inferred from these facts that *rāṣaḥ* means a particular kind of killing. It is different from what the Old Testament law demands in particular cases and also from what could be commanded in war. This seems to make it likely that the meaning of *rāṣaḥ* was 'murder', so that those who render the commandment 'You shall not murder' would be shown to be right. This, however, is not the case. Certainly *rāṣaḥ* often does mean 'murder', but it is also used besides this in speaking of the man who kills another unintentionally.[68] *rāṣaḥ* shows itself to be a definite concept of the Hebrew language, the meaning of which cannot be confined to the alternatives killing/murdering. What *rāṣaḥ* means in contrast to *hārag* and *hēmīt* is illegal killing inimical to the community. If one wanted to find a concise expression for the rendering of the commandment, then 'You shall not commit manslaughter' could be considered. But that is not really adequate. It will therefore be better to keep to the accustomed 'You shall not kill' which now has to be clarified along the lines that the life of the Israelite was protected in this way from illegal impermissible violence. The commandment thus has its place in a community in which capital punishment exists and war is permitted or even sometimes commanded. The concept of killing inimical to the community is unambiguous in the Old Testament since Israel was at one and the same time people and community. The New Testament only knows the community, the community consisting of many peoples. How is the concept of that which is inimical to the community to be determined here? That is the question for Christian ethics, and the answer must be sought between the words of Jesus in the Sermon on the Mount (Matt. 5.21 ff) and the Pauline doctrine of the state.

[68] Thus in the passages: Deut. 4.41–43; 19.1–13; Num. 35; Josh. 20 and 21.

8. *'You shall not commit adultery'*

In connection with this commandment, Otto Procksch[69] draws attention to the fact that there is nothing here about monogamy or polygamy, or about blood and tribal relationships. The prohibition of adultery does, however, presuppose a legitimate marriage, the understanding of which can be refined and altered in the course of time. 'The ancient character of the Decalogue means that we are to understand from it that the man can only commit adultery against a marriage other than his own, the woman only against her own.' Procksch refers to Bernhard Stade[70] in order to give the reason for this sentence. Here it is stated: 'Intercourse of the man outside the marriage with unmarried and unbetrothed women gives no offence (Gen. 38; Judg. 16), and the seduction of an unbetrothed daughter of a family is an offence against property (Ex. 22.15 f). Only the wife and the betrothed woman are bound to faithfulness; the man can commit adultery only against the marriage of another man (Gen. 39.10 ff). . . .' As has already been remarked, the commandment, with its general formulation, is not bound to a particular ancient order of society. It was thus able to go along with a changing conception of marriage which was becoming more refined. It can be seen from the warnings of the Book of Proverbs against adultery and unchastity[71] that Israel's development in this matter did not stop here. This is especially the case with the warning against the 'strange woman' (ch. 5), by whom is meant not a foreigner, but a married Israelite, who is described as a strange woman inasmuch as she belongs to another man.[72]

Reventlow takes pains to go more deeply into the understanding of the commandment.[73] In doing this, he emphasizes its representative character; the committing of adultery brought into view the whole field of sexuality, 'which, with its many varied temptations, brought with it a particularly acute danger for a way of life conformable to the faith of Yahweh'.

[69] *Theologie des Alten Testaments*, p. 88.
[70] *Biblische Theologie des Alten Testaments* I, p. 199.
[71] Especially in chs. 5, 6 and 7, but also in 22.14; 23.26–28; 29.3; 30.20; 31.3.
[72] On this, see Paul Humbert, 'La "femme étrangère" du livre des Proverbes', *Revue des Études Sémitiques*, 1937, pp. 49–64.
[73] *Gebot und Predigt*, pp. 77 ff.

ADDITIONS

Von Rad[74] notes that the man was permitted intercourse with the female slaves of his house, but this type of marriage was also protected by strict legal forms, the disregard of which counted as adultery. This kind of marriage cannot be called monogamous, but still less can it simply be called polygamous.

9. 'You shall not steal. You shall not covet'

These two commandments are taken together for reasons which will shortly become clear. In the case of the eighth, it is almost universally accepted that it has been handed down in its original form. Rabast, whose reconstruction we have already met,[75] makes an exception to this. His reconstruction reads: 'You shall not steal a man or a woman.' We can at once understand the presuppositions of this attempt, and acknowledge that it is partly correct, though in part it will have to be criticized. The original form of the tenth commandment was no doubt as follows: 'You shall not covet your neighbour's house.' This was later supplemented, as it seems, in two stages. In the first, there was added: 'You shall not covet your neighbour's wife, or his manservant, or his maidservant, or his ox, or his ass', and in the second: 'or any thing which is your neighbour's.' The first of the two additions defines somewhat more closely the property involved (which was first only designated by the word 'house') by enumerating individual possessions, while the second, in a general formulation, embraces the property in its entirety. Its general nature shows it to be the latest element of all.[76]

The prevailing opinion about the tenth commandment is that it has the covetous will, that is, an offence of the mind, in view. This can find support in the Greek rendering in the Septuagint which offers in both Ex. 20 and Deut. 5 *ouk epithumeseis* (twice each); it has the authority of Luther behind it,[77] and it is advocated

---

[74] *Deuteronomy*, p. 59.

[75] See above, p. 20.

[76] For this reason, it was not a happy idea of Hans Schmidt, 'Mose und der Dekalog', *EHG*, pp. 82 and 91–93, to look for the oldest part of the commandment in this of all its elements.

[77] He declares in the Longer Catechism that the commandment is 'directed particularly against envy and loathsome avarice'.

both by the moral theologian Alfred de Quervain[78] and also by the exegetes Paul Volz[79] and Georg Beer.[80] But is it correct? Would the Decalogue, in its own original ancient form, really have forbidden the false thought, the covetous impulse of the heart? It is not likely. It brings up the question concerning the meaning of the verb *ḥāmad* which occurs twice in the text of Ex. 20, while in that of Deut. 5, *hit'awwā* is used for it once. Both verbs mean 'covet', yet there are two of them, so that it is to be presumed that, at least originally, they were distinguished by different shades of meaning. This difference, which was long unrecognized or at the most surmised,[81] was discovered by Johannes Herrmann and presented in 1927 in an article on the tenth commandment.[82] As well as Alt,[83] Koehler has also acknowledged the result in his account of research.[84] Herrmann first draws attention to the fact that the verb *ḥāmad* is repeatedly followed in the Old Testament by verbs which mean as much as 'take' or 'rob'. Thus in Deut. 7.25 the Israelites are not to covet (*ḥāmad*) the gold and silver that is on the images of the Canaanite gods, and take it for themselves. This is the case also in Josh. 7.21, in Achan's confession of guilt. He names the seductive pieces of booty and concludes: 'then I coveted them, and took them' (*wā'eḥmᵉdēm wā'eqqāḥēm*). Finally, in Micah 2.2, the prophet pillories the avaricious rich with the words: 'They covet (*ḥāmᵉdu*) fields and seize them; and houses, and take them away.' Herrmann concludes from these passages[85] that 'evidently the Hebrew understood *ḥāmad* to mean an emotion which with a certain necessity leads to corresponding actions'. The correctness of this is confirmed by two further passages which, however, go further than those already mentioned, since, after *ḥāmad*, they have no following verb which supplements it and expresses the taking possession of the thing coveted. The first of these is Ps. 68.16 which reads: 'Why look you with envy,

[78] In his book: *Das Gesetz Gottes. Die zweite Tafel*, Munich, 1936, pp. 51 ff.
[79] *Mose und sein Werk*, 2nd ed., Tübingen, 1932, pp. 54 f.
[80] *Exodus*, Tübingen, 1939, p. 103.
[81] Thus Eerdmans in 'Ursprung und Bedeutung der Zehn Worte', *ThT* 37, 1903, pp. 19 ff, especially p. 25, where *lō'-taḥmōd* is translated: 'You shall not appropriate to yourself that which is without owner' (*du sollst dir das Herrenlose nicht zueignen*). See also Eerdmans, *The Religion of Israel*, Leiden, 1947, p. 31.
[82] 'Das zehnte Gebot', *Sellin-Festschrift*, Leipzig, 1927, pp. 69–82.
[83] 'Das Verbot des Diebstahls im Dekalog', *KS* I, pp. 333 f.
[84] 'Der Dekalog', *ThR*, NS 1, 1929, p. 183.
[85] *Op. cit.*, p. 72.

O many-peaked mountain, at the mount which God desired for his abode, yea, where Yahweh will dwell for ever?' The wording assumes that it is not a matter of desiring (*ḥāmad*) alone, but also of attainment, which, for that reason, is not specially brought out with a second verb. The second passage (Ex. 34.24) reads: 'For I will cast out nations before you, and enlarge your borders; neither shall any man desire your land, when you go up to appear before Yahweh your God three times in the year.' The text contains the promise that Yahweh, in the time of the three annual pilgrimages, when there are no men on the frontiers, will keep the land free from hostile attack. The words 'neither shall any man desire your land' clearly express the invasion which followed the coveting.

All the passages named show that *ḥāmad* does not only mean 'covet' as an impulse of the will, but that it also includes the intrigues which lead to the taking possession of that which was coveted. This will also be true for the tenth commandment. According to its original meaning then, it does not only aim at the will, but simultaneously at the violent intrigues which a person uses in order to attain to the property of his neighbour. A confirmation of what can be gathered from the Hebrew language concerning the meaning of *ḥāmad* comes from a recent discovery to which Alt has drawn attention.[86] After the Second World War, Old Phoenician inscriptions were discovered in the border country between Cilicia and Syria, near the locality called Karatepe, in which the verb *ḥāmad* is used of the action of a foreign king or ruler who was to try to put himself into possession of a newly-built city. We quote: 'Or if he [that is, the foreign king] covets this city and tears down this door. . . .'[87]

From the point of view of language, Herrmann's insight cannot be contested. It was, however, long encumbered with the great difficulty of fixing its limits over against the eighth commandment. This seemed to be impossible if the tenth also had to do with actual theft. Consideration of this caused Volz and Beer[88] to

---

[86] *KS* I, p. 334, n. 1.

[87] Alt, 'Die phönikischen Inschriften von Karatepe', *Die Welt des Orients* I, 1947–52, pp. 274 f and 278 f. [See also *ANET*, pp. 500a f, where Franz Rosenthal offers a somewhat different translation. Tr.] In Ugaritic too the root *ḥ m d* seems to have had the shade of meaning which Herrmann inferred for Hebrew, as for instance in a passage of the text no. 75 (in John Gray, *The Legacy of Canaan*, Leiden, 1957, p. 65, l. 15).

[88] See above, p. 102, nn. 79 and 80.

reject the view of Herrmann, and to continue to limit *ḥāmad*, as was done before, to purely mental coveting. One authority stands against the other—how is one to decide? Once again Albrecht Alt has shown the way in an article written in 1949.[89] He has demonstrated that the eighth commandment originally had in view not theft in general, but kidnapping (the stealing of persons), and still more accurately, not the kidnapping of any person, but only that of the free Israelite man. The waylaying of dependent persons or those who were not free, such as women, children and slaves, is on the other hand covered by the tenth commandment. This is a differentiation which Rabast neglects when, for the sake of metrical balance, he finds the oldest wording of the commandment in the sentence: 'You shall not steal a man or *a woman.*'

It is with special reference to Ex. 21.16 and Deut. 24.7 that Alt provides the proof for his thesis. They both have the prohibition of kidnapping as their content, and the first belongs to a series of apodictic clauses, from which it follows that the transgression mentioned belonged to the subject matter of apodictic law, so that it can also have its place in the Decalogue. It is not until this understanding of the eighth commandment has been reached that the inner connection between the five last clauses of the Decalogue is properly illuminated, since it can then be seen that each of them ensures a fundamental right of the free Israelite citizen. Beginning with the sixth commandment, they are: his life, his marriage, his freedom, his reputation and his property.

In the course of time, the meaning of the eighth commandment, which has certainly been inferred correctly, lost its original distinctive meaning, probably as a result of the tenth commandment coming to be thought of only in connection with mental coveting. This development starts in the Old Testament itself, that is, in Deuteronomy, which, as pointed out earlier,[90] replaces the second *lō'-taḥmōd* 'you shall not covet' by a *lō' tit'awwe*, and thus interprets the preceding verb in a particular direction. The direction is that towards mental coveting, for such a coveting is expressed by the verb *hit'-awwā*. As distinct from *ḥāmad*, this means coveting only in the sense of an impulse of the will, without the measures which lead to the realization of the wish being included. This can be seen in passages where (in contrast with *ḥāmad*) the

---

[89] 'Das Verbot des Diebstahls im Dekalog', *KS* I, pp. 333–340.
[90] See above, p. 14.

day of Yahweh or the day of disaster appear as the object of the
desire (Amos 5.18; Jer. 17.16), objects for whose attainment
human means are in any case useless. This is also true of Isa.
26.9: 'My soul yearns for thee in the night, my spirit within me
earnestly seeks thee.'

It is certainly relevant to know that the interpretation of the
tenth commandment which was carried further in the Septuagint,
and which was taken up by Christian exegesis, already had its
beginnings in the Old Testament itself.

ADDITIONS

Berend Maarsingh[91] offers a very pictorial definition of *ḥāmad*
which he has taken from Th. C. Vriezen.[92] The verb is rendered by
haken naar, *de haak uitslaan naar*, literally, 'to put one's hook out
after'. Where the neighbour's wife is mentioned, as in Deut. 5.21,
the text is concerned to forbid efforts to put her into one's own
power.

Hans Joachim Stoebe,[93] however, is not so sure about this
meaning of *ḥāmad*. In the case of Micah 2.2, he asks whether the
context from v. 1 does not rather show that it is a matter of the
swiftness of the deed than of the inner logic of the happening.
Ex. 34.24 is understood as follows: nobody would think of doing
what is mentioned here, for the order set by Yahweh is so sure and
holy that it cannot even be questioned by a thought. As far as the
eighth commandment is concerned, he considers the formulation to be purely apodictic and so wide that it includes all conceivable kinds of stealing. This latter presupposes that apodictic
law must be universal in this sense, which is by no means
necessarily the case, and of the other two considerations presented,
the second, on Ex. 34.24 is not very convincing. That of Micah
2.2 is more so, though there is still the question of the other
passages mentioned by Stamm above. The reference to the context of Micah 2.2 is, however, important, because it reminds us
that, in the search for the meaning of a word, one has to consider

[91] *Onderzoek naar de Ethiek van de Wetten in Deuteronomium* (with a summary
in English), Winterswijk, 1961, pp. 65 and 118.
[92] *Hoofdlijnen der Theologie van het Oude Testament*, Wageningen, 1949, p. 274
(cf. *An Outline of Old Testament Theology*, ETr., Oxford, 1958, pp. 330 f).
[93] 'Das achte Gebot (Exod. 20, Vers 16)', *WuD*, NS 3, 1952, pp. 110 and
126.

not only the context of the passage being used, but also whether the meaning then found fits into the context of the passage to which one wishes to apply it[94]—in this case the Decalogue. The difficulty with the latter is that there is so little, at least of an exterior nature, to go by; this means that the greatest caution is called for. This would also apply to the other commandments where word meanings have been brought into consideration. In the cases which have been considered, it can at least be said that the meanings found would probably fit into the original context of the commandments of the Decalogue in the ethos of the clan. But this does not mean, on the other hand, that other meanings would not be possible, and in the investigations of the meanings of words, it sometimes happens that it is the question whether the meaning found fits into the appropriate clause of the Decalogue, or into the Decalogue as a whole, which is given the least attention.

As far as *gānab* 'steal' is concerned, one can have doubts about the meaning which Alt has postulated for it, for, of the passages to which he draws special attention, Ex. 21.16 and Deut. 24.7, not even the first belongs to the prohibitions in Gerstenberger's sense, and even if they did, the fact that one meaning can be found for one apodictic series, does not necessarily mean that another apodictic series will have the same meaning. Alt's meaning for *gānab* is, as a matter of fact, doubted by Gerstenberger.[95] He thinks that its occurrence in passages where small groups of prohibited actions are mentioned (Ex. 20.13–15; [21.15–17]; Josh. 7.11; Jer. 7.9; Hos. 4.2) speaks decisively against the restricted meaning which Alt gives it. This may not necessarily be the case, but certainly Alt's argumentation from the series of 'apodictic' law is not decisive either. Unfortunately none of this leads to any definite conclusion for the reader (or for the writer!), but it does seem necessary to add a word of caution.

C. H. Gordon[96] thinks that the reason for the prohibition in the tenth commandment is the same as that for many prohibitions in the Old Testament—it stems from opposition to Canaanite religion. It is not because coveting is immoral or illegal that it is

[94] See James Barr, *The Semantics of Biblical Language*, Oxford, 1961.

[95] Diss., p. 72 and n. 240. We have already referred to his doubts about the original form being short, i.e. without an object (see above, p. 21).

[96] 'A Note on the Tenth Commandment', *The Journal of Bible and Religion* 31, 1963, pp. 208–209. For another article by Gordon, see also now, 'The Ten Commandments', *Christianity Today* 8, 1964, pp. 625–628.

prohibited, but because Baal (as can be seen from Ugaritic texts) coveted (*ḥāmad*) bull, field and house. It is not completely impossible that this was the motivation for the prohibition in the first place, though if the tenth commandment had its origin in nomadic times, it becomes less likely. Further, one reason which Gordon seems to imply as a support for his explanation from the background of opposition to the usage of Israel's neighbours, namely that no one has ever proposed that people be punished for coveting, falls away if it is accepted that it belongs to the essence of apodictic law that it does not stipulate a punishment. This being so, it is not necessary to state a punishment to show that what is prohibited is immoral or illegal. In any case, if *ḥamad* means the desire together with the intrigues which lead to the taking possession of the thing desired, a punishment *could* very well be proposed for this. Quite apart from this, an objection stemming from the consideration of the importance of relation to the context seems to be in order here too: just because it can be shown that Baal coveted, this does not by itself mean that that was the reason why coveting was prohibited in the Decalogue.

10. 'You shall not bear false witness'

The Exodus version of this commandment reads in Hebrew: *lō'-taʿᵃne bᵉrēʿᵃkā ʿēd šāqer*, which, translated literally, means: 'You shall not answer against your neighbour as a lying witness.' In Deuteronomy, the commandment reads: *lō'-taʿᵃne bᵉrēʿᵃkā ʿēd šāw'*, 'You shall not answer against your neighbour as a witness of emptiness.' The words *šeqer*, 'lie', and *šāw'*, 'that which is vain', 'empty', 'transitory', are similar in Hebrew without, however, being completely identical, since *šeqer* means primarily 'lie', 'deceit', and then, developing from there, 'that which is delusive', 'pointless', whereas it is just the other way around with *šāw'*. Here the meaning 'vain', 'without any purpose' will have stood at the beginning, and that of 'lying', 'without any foundation' will have come to it subsequently. If the words are similar in content but still not identical, then we must enquire which of the two expressions *ʿēd šeqer* or *ʿēd šāw'* was the original one in the Decalogue. The answer which is to be given unhesitatingly to this question (it has already been touched on above[97]), is that *ʿēd šeqer* must be considered as the original wording, and that it was then given a supplementing interpretation by the deuteronomic version. Every false statement was to be forbidden, and no one was to be able to claim that he had not actually told a lie. The reason why ʿēd šeqer is to be preferred as the oldest is because it is an expression which can also be found in the Old Testament outside the Decalogue (Ps. 27.12; Prov. 6.19; 12.17; 14.5; 19.5,9; 25.18); it thus shows itself to be a set expression. ʿēd šāwʾ, on the other hand, is to be found only in the deuteronomic version of the Decalogue, which permits the conclusion that it is a reformulation of the old expression.

The expression 'lying witness' leads us into the sphere of legal language, to which the verb used in the commandment— Hebrew ʿānā—also belongs. In addition to the frequent meaning 'answer', this also has a special meaning, since it is a technical term for the reciprocal 'answering' of the parties in law. It is found frequently in this sense in the Book of Job, and also in the well-known controversy in Micah (6.1–8), where Yahweh, speaking first in the function of the accused (v. 3), summons the people standing against him as plaintiff to bring forward their grievances: 'O my people, what have I done to you? In what have I wearied you? Answer me!' (ʿanē bī). In the context of legal language, the verb ʿānā could be used in particular as the term for the testimony before the judges and the parties. As an example of this, we mention only the passage Num. 35.30: 'no person shall be put to death on the testimony of one witness.' The ninth commandment is directly related to this; it has the same strictly legal use of the verb.

Ludwig Koehler[98] has drawn attention to the surprising fact that the Decalogue does not contain any prohibition of lying.[99] As is known, it has often been thought possible to fill up this omission in the ninth commandment. This is the case in Luther's Shorter Catechism, where the commandment is brought into connection with lying, calumny and slander. This certainly does not correspond to the original meaning, since this, being bound to a particular situation in Israelite life, is much less extensive and universal. The free Israelite had certain basic obligations; besides those relating to the cult and to war, he also had obligations in

[98] L. Koehler, *Old Testament Theology*, ETr., London, 1957, p. 202.
[99] On the lie in the Old Testament, see also now M. A. Klopfenstein, *Die Lüge nach dem Alten Testament*, Zürich, 1964.

relation to the administration of justice. As is known from Ruth 4 and Jer. 26, every citizen could be involved in this. When such a case came up, it could catch him unexpectedly, as he was on his way to work. Israelite law was in large part handled by ordinary people, local men who functioned as judges and appeared as witnesses.

It is in accordance with the importance of this task that the Decalogue contains a prohibition, not of lying, but of false witness. We have just said[100] that it is a characteristic that, in each of its last five commandments, it protects *one* of the basic rights of the Israelite. The matter involved in the ninth commandment is his reputation, and this was much more directly preserved by the concrete prohibition of false witness than by a general proscription of the lie. In addition to this, the court of law was the situation in which truth and falsehood were of particular importance. It was the place from which the blessing of truth and the corruption of falsehood originated and from where it spread to the people. He who showed himself to be truthful here would not have wanted to give way to falsehood elsewhere. It is therefore tempting to speak of the commandment having a paradigmatic character. In the way in which it is expressed, it shows just how important the Hebrew's neighbour was to him in the question of truth—no less than in other spheres of life. It is not a question here of truth as a matter of mere personal thinking and of behaviour in private, but of its public manifestation in relation to one's brother.

It is quite clear to everyone who is acquainted with the original text that the ninth commandment refers exclusively to witness in the court of law, and not to lying in general as well. This must always be taken into account in the face of an over-hasty exposition of the commandment in relation to lying. Every theologian has the task of opening up the original meaning of the commandment to his hearers, of whatever age they might be, and of awakening in them the understanding of the particular form in which it has been given to us. The extension of the commandment to the sphere of lying must take place only secondarily. But here it may be done with a good conscience, and not only because false witness itself is an extreme particular case of lying, but also for the reason that the Old Testament, when it designates the false

[100] See above, p. 104.

witness frequently as lying witness,[101] has seen the essence of the
false witness in the lie itself.

ADDITIONS

Stamm himself has pointed out above that the words *šeqer* and
šāw' are similar in Hebrew, though he maintains that the meaning
'lie' is primary for the first, while 'vain' is primary for the second.
Stoebe, however, when discussing Deuteronomy's replacement
of '*ed šeqer* of Ex. 20.16 with '*ed šāw'*,[102] regards *šāw'* as a synonym
for *šeqer* in Hos. 10.4, and finds it difficult to decide which of the
two is original in the Decalogue. He thinks, however, that, as far
as *šāw'*, in general is concerned, its meaning as that which is
lying and ignoble is undoubtedly secondary to its meaning as that
which is empty and transitory. M. E. Andrew, in two essays,[103] has
also indicated that these two words can both be used in the sense
of both lying and emptiness, but it is not proved that *in Ex. 20
and Deut. 5* both words are meant in both senses. It could mean,
however, that *šāw'* in Deuteronomy is not necessarily more precise in meaning, but was simply the natural word for Deuteronomy to choose as the equivalent of *šeqer*, and perhaps that both
šeqer and *šāw'* in the two passages carried the double meaning of
lying and emptiness—or, at least, came to carry it.

Stoebe[104] is also concerned to show the connection between this
commandment and two others, namely the third and the eighth
(for him, the second and the seventh). The missing reference to the
lie can be found in Hos. 4.2 and Jer. 7.9, and it is characteristic
that, in both cases, they have a form which reminds us of the
third rather than the ninth commandment. This is because the
misuse of the name of Yahweh includes false oaths as well as curse
and sorcery. In Ex. 22.7, the prohibition of swearing falsely comes
so close to that of stealing that it seems to be judged as nothing
less than an extension of the latter. In Ex. 22.12, the witness has
to speak what he knows before God, and this makes it clear why
the demand of the ninth commandment can be subordinated to
that of the third and can be taken up into it.

[101] See above, p. 108.
[102] 'Das achte Gebot', *WuD*, NS 3, 1952, p. 114.
[103] 'Using God: Ex. 20.7', *ExpT* 74, 1962–63, pp. 304–307; 'Falsehood and
Truth: Ex. 20:16', *Interpretation* 17, 1963, pp. 425–438, especially p. 433.
[104] *Op. cit.*, pp. 114 ff.

The implication of this would be that all three commandments come to basically the same thing. Taking God's name in vain, stealing, and false witness all represent using God and one's neighbour for one's own purposes.[105]

Maarsingh[106] says that no categorical prohibition is known from extra-biblical law books which is formulated just as it is in Deut. 5.20 and Ex. 20.16, that is, a prohibition against appearing as a witness whose statement is empty or based on falsehood.

Von Rad[107] points out that this commandment was so important because, in Israelite law, very great significance attached to the testimony of the witness, seeing that the responsibility for proof lay with the accused; he had to prove his innocence of the charge.

[105] For a consideration of other views of Stoebe on this commandment, especially that it is not originally confined to the context of the law-court, and that *'ēd* belongs to sacral law, see Stamm's criticism in his more detailed article, 'Dreissig Jahre Dekalogforschung', *ThR*, NS 27, 1961, pp. 300 f.

[106] *Onderzoek naar de Ethiek van de Wetten in Deuteronomium*, p. 30.

[107] *Deuteronomy*, p. 59.

III

CONCLUSION

HAVING treated the Ten Commandments individually above, we now in this summing-up turn to the question of the distinctive character of the Decalogue within the world of the various religions. But if we take the commandments which have to do with the relationship with one's neighbour, beginning with the commandment about parents, they do not show this distinctive character. There are numerous parallels to these commandments among primitive peoples, as Nathan Söderblom has shown,[1] and similar parallels can also be brought forward from among Israel's neighbours in the ancient Near East. In Egypt they can be found in the Book of the Dead (ch. 125), and in Babylon in a section of a large collection of incantations.[2] In both texts transgressions which a person could have committed are listed, and among them are some which agree exactly with those which are forbidden in the Decalogue, from the fifth to the tenth commandments. We can even say that, in the Egyptian Book of the Dead, the refinement of moral judgement has perhaps advanced even further, since here the sins which were not committed by the deceased include not only killing but also inciting to kill. Lying is also present in the catalogue of sins avoided. When making comparisons with Israel, however, we cannot overlook the fact that the agreements with the Decalogue are limited to individual clauses within long lists of transgressions. We look in vain in Egypt and in Babylon for a concise compilation of central prohibitions; neither can we find in

[1] *Das Werden des Gottesglaubens*, Leipzig, 1916 (2nd ed., 1926), pp. 147 f.
[2] German translations of these texts are to be found in Hugo Gressmann, *Altorientalische Texte zum Alten Testament*, 2nd ed., Berlin, 1926, pp. 10 ff and 324 f. For the section from the Egyptian Book of the Dead see also J. H. Breasted, *The Dawn of Conscience*, New York, 1933, pp. 263 ff. [An English translation of parts of ch. 125 of the Book of the Dead can be found in *ANET*, pp. 34a ff. Tr.]

either country a festival at which the reading out of short legal maxims formed the central feature.

This brings us to the introduction to the Decalogue which was bound up with the festival in a special way, and to the first four commandments. While the introduction which takes up the history of salvation is also without parallel, the first four commandments are not quite in the same position. In the Babylonian text mentioned, the contempt of a god or a goddess is included among the transgressions which could have brought down the divine curse, and according to the Book of the Dead, the Egyptian confesses that he has not committed anything which is abominable to the gods. The commandment concerning the sabbath awakes a distant echo of the Assyrian prescriptions concerned with the taboo days. But all the comparisons which can be made between ancient Near Eastern material and the opening commandments only brings out all the more clearly the distance at which Israel stood from its environment. Certainly, there were duties towards the gods in Babylon and in Egypt which it was not permitted to neglect. What does not exist however—apart from the episode of Akhenaton in Egypt—is the exclusiveness in the worship of God, and, connected with this, the prohibition of apostasy.[3] For Babylonian and Egyptian thinking, a prohibition of images was not possible either. The very case of Akhenaton itself shows this; he allowed the validity of nothing more than a sober representation of the sun god, and proscribed the traditional modes of representation together with the images of the remaining gods. This was an irreverent radicalism which, according to the experts, contributed much to the hatred which, after the death of the heretical king, erupted against his movement. Israel was placed under the exclusive claim of the divine Lord of the Covenant, and was directed towards his word and not his image, a stranger among her neighbours both great and small. In this foreignness, she went her way from a particular beginning towards a goal. The beginning springs from the deliverance from Egypt and the events on Sinai, or in Kadesh, to which the proclamation of the Decalogue belonged. Within the practice of the Israelite cult, it always stood in the light of these events. For this reason, it was not given the name of law, nor was it understood as such. The

---

[3] On the prohibition of apostasy as the main characteristic of Old Testament law, see M. Noth, 'Die Gesetze im Pentateuch', *GSAT*, pp. 70 ff.

Decalogue was the charter of freedom which Yahweh had presented to his people delivered from Egypt. The people received it not as a burden, but as a gift, which was seen as a privilege and as an occasion for thanks. We thus see that what gives the Decalogue its special position in the history of religion is only in part its content (though this part was significant); its significance was, above all, in the position which, from the earliest times on, it came to occupy in the life of ancient Israel.

INDEX OF NAMES

INDEX OF BIBLICAL REFERENCES